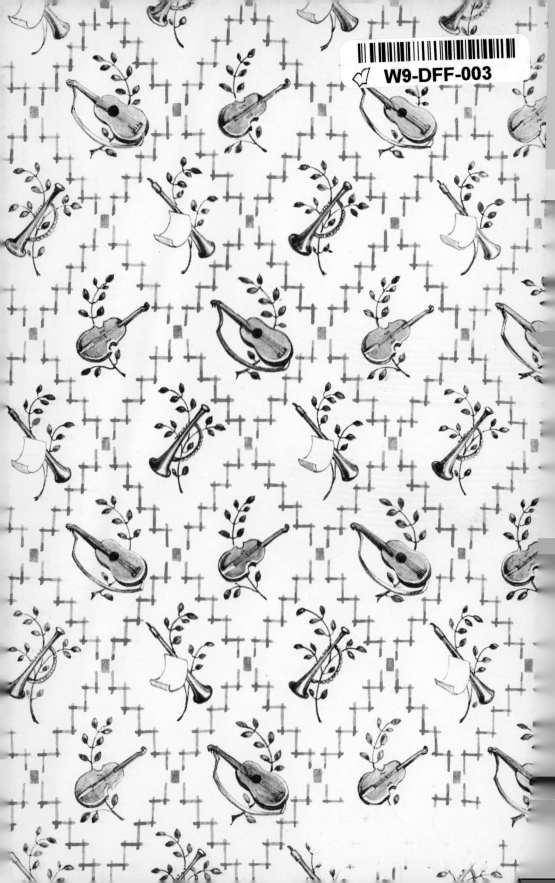

UNFINISHED SYMPHONY
The Story of Franz Schubert

Books by Madeleine Goss

BEETHOVEN, MASTER MUSICIAN
DEEP-FLOWING BROOK: *The Story of Johann Sebastian Bach*
BOLERO: *The Life of Maurice Ravel*
UNFINISHED SYMPHONY: *The Story of Franz Schubert*

FRANZ
SCHUBERT

UNFINISHED SYMPHONY

SYMPHONY

The Story of Franz Schubert

By MADELEINE GOSS

Illustrated by KARL M. SCHULTHEISS

NEW YORK

HENRY HOLT AND COMPANY

PRINTED IN THE
UNITED STATES OF AMERICA

"When I wished to sing of love, it turned into sorrow; and when I wanted to sing of sorrow, it was transformed for me into love."

—Franz Schubert, *My Dream*

ACKNOWLEDGMENTS

In gathering material for this volume, the author acknowledges especial indebtedness to the researches of Walter Newman Flower (*Franz Schubert: The Man and His Circle*, Stokes, 1928), and of Karl Kobald (*Franz Schubert and His Times*, transl. by Beatrice Marshall, Knopf, 1928); and thanks the publishers for permission to quote a number of anecdotes and translations found in these books. Acknowledgment is also made to Alfred Knopf, publisher of *Franz Schubert's Letters and Other Writings*, for the privilege of reproducing certain of Schubert's letters and excerpts from his diary, contained in the German edition of this work (edited by Otto Erich Deutsch), and in the English translation by Venetia Savile.

Special appreciation is due Mrs. Elizabeth C. Moore for her help in editing the manuscript, in compiling the index and list of compositions, and in preparing the contemporary chart entitled "The World That Schubert Lived In."

CONTENTS

CHAPTER   PAGE

I THE "KONVIKT" SCHOOL I

II FATHER SCHUBERT 17

III AT THE SIGN OF THE BLACK HORSE 34

IV MUSIC COMES FIRST 49

V NAPOLEON THE CONQUEROR 65

VI FRANZ IN DISGRACE 79

VII ANOTHER SCHOOLMASTER? 98

VIII FRANZ FALLS IN LOVE 115

IX THE ERL-KING 134

X FREEDOM—AT ANY PRICE! 149

XI COUNT ESTERHÁZY AND HIS FAMILY 165

XII "VIENNA—BELOVED VIENNA!" 182

XIII A TRIP TO UPPER AUSTRIA 197

XIV "SCHUBERTIADES" 217

XV "MY DREAM" 237

XVI MOONSHINE HOUSE 255

XVII "TO HIM WHO WILL BE NEXT" 272

XVIII WITH BEETHOVEN 288

THE WORLD THAT SCHUBERT LIVED IN . . . 296

FRANZ SCHUBERT'S COMPOSITIONS 299

READING LIST 304

INDEX 305

The reader who is interested in more of the facts
and data on Schubert's life will find a rewarding
section of supplementary material at the back of
the book. There is a chart which relates the hap-
penings in Schubert's life with the other musical,
and non-musical, events of the time. There is a
list of Schubert's compositions, a reading list of
books related to the story of Franz Schubert's life,
and an index suitable for use by young readers.

CHAPTER I

The "Konvikt" School

HERR DIREKTOR LANG looked over the row of anxious-faced contestants who sat before the judges in the Music Room of the Konvikt School in Vienna.

"Next?" he called.

A small, stout boy rose reluctantly and stumbled over to the platform. He was in an agony of self-consciousness; the whole roomful of people, he knew, was staring at his back!—those other boys in the front row, all hoping to be chosen for the Imperial Choir, their parents and friends behind them, and in the very back the mocking Konvikt students.

I

Director Lang, principal of the school and chief examiner, was a tall, stern man with a flowing black beard. He looked appraisingly at the boy who stood before him, and thought to himself: "Not a very likely candidate!"

The child was short and round-faced, with unruly brown curls and a deep dimple in his chin. He wore large, steel-rimmed spectacles that gave him an unnaturally solemn expression, and made his stout figure seem somehow ridiculous. He was dressed in a faded blue smock and heavy, worn boots.

"What is your name?" Herr Lang asked.

"Sch-Schubert, sir," the boy answered in a low voice. "Franz Peter Seraph Schubert."

"Speak up!" the Director complained. "I can hardly hear you. When were you born—and where?"

"January 31st, sir, 1797," Franz stammered, "in Lichtenthal, just outside the walls of Vienna."

"Hum-m-m," said Herr Lang, making a rapid mental calculation. "That makes you eleven, going on twelve. You don't look so old as that. What is your father's name?"

"Franz Theodor Schubert." The boy wished desperately that his father could have been there to help him through this ordeal. Herr Schubert had accompanied his son as far as the Konvikt, but then he had been obliged to return to his own school.

"I wonder if you realize, Franz, what it will mean to us if you pass the examinations," his father had said to him on the long walk over from Lichtenthal early that morning. "It is of course an honor to be admitted to the Imperial Choir, but much more important is the scholarship that goes with it. Your future will be assured if you can get into the Konvikt School. Otherwise," he continued as if to himself, "I don't know how we could manage to give you a proper education. . . ."

But Franz was only half listening to his father; for suddenly, in the middle of the street (these inspirations were likely to occur to him in the most unexpected places!), a beautiful new tune had flashed through his mind. It expressed just what was in his heart—all his feelings about the gay September morning and the excitement of this new adventure, things that he felt but never could have said in words. Should he write it in minuet form? . . . in the key of G, or . . .

"Watch where you are going, young man!" his father cried sharply. Franz came back to earth just as he was about to step into a large mud-puddle. "Dreaming again!" Herr Schubert scolded. "They won't put up with that sort of thing at the Konvikt. You must learn to depend on yourself now."

Franz, remembering his father's words, pulled himself up and faced the judges.

"What is your father's profession?" the Director was asking.

There was a suppressed titter at the back of the room. Franz imagined he could hear the Konvikt students whispering: "He's a miller's son, that new boy—see if he isn't!"

"Silence!" roared Director Lang.

There was instant quiet in the room, as Franz replied with a certain pride: "My father is Headmaster at the Lichtenthal school."

He looked down at his faded blue smock. Earlier that morning the boys had made fun of it. . . .

Franz recalled how cold and forbidding the school had looked as he stood on the doorstep, trying to make up his mind to ring the bell. When at last he timidly pulled at the shiny brass handle, the sound echoed through the building with such a lugubrious clang that he wanted to take to his heels.

But before he could collect his wits, the door was opened by a stupid-looking maid.

"Please, Fräulein," Franz stammered, "I have come for the examinations."

The girl looked at him doubtfully. "Examinations—? Oh, yes, for the Imperial Choir. But they don't begin until nine-thirty." She half closed the door, then opened it again. "I suppose since you are here you might as well come in and wait."

She ushered him into a dark, draughty passage-way. Everything at the Konvikt seemed cold and gloomy; the rooms were small and poorly lighted by high, narrow windows. Franz felt chilled to the bone by the inhospitable atmosphere.

As he waited in the stone-paved corridor, he heard a rush of feet and saw some boys peering at him from a doorway. They stared at Franz impudently.

"Just in from the country!" one of the boys tittered, as he examined the newcomer's shrinking figure.

A stout lad with red cheeks pushed forward and boldly fingered the faded smock. "Looks as if it had flour on it," he said with a burst of merry laughter. "He must be a miller's son!"

"*Ja, ja,* Holzapfel, a miller's son—a nice fat miller's son . . ." the group began to chant, dancing around poor Franz.

Young Schubert would have given anything to escape from his tormentors, but he managed somehow to keep a smile on his round, friendly face. Fortunately at that moment a tall youth of nineteen or twenty came striding down the hall.

"What's going on here, you young savages? Whom are you teasing now?" he cried.

The boys immediately stood to one side. "It's

a new boy, Herr Spaun," they said. "He's come for the examinations."

"Well, he doesn't have to wait here in the hall. Take him up to the Music Room—you, Holzapfel!"

The red-cheeked boy seemed quite friendly as he led the way up a flight of stone steps. Franz thought that the name "Wooden-Apple" suited him well.

Holzapfel took the newcomer to a large room at the end of the corridor on the second floor. Benches and chairs had been placed in readiness for the coming auditions, and there were special seats for the judges on a platform.

"You will have quite a wait," said "Wooden-Apple" as he turned to go back to his comrades.

But Franz didn't mind. As soon as he was left alone he fumbled in his pocket for a bit of paper and a stubby pencil. Seating himself on a corner of one of the benches, he began to write down the melody that had flashed into his mind on his way to the Konvikt. He was still writing when the other contestants began to come in.

Only the finest boy-singers of Vienna were taken into the Imperial Choir of the Royal Chapel. Each Sunday, and on special feast days and other occasions, they sang for the Emperor and his family, and members of the Austrian Court.   In return for their services they were given free scholarships at the Konvikt. This was an old Jesuit school, one of the best in Vienna, and had nothing to do with a prison, as the name might seem to indicate.

Whenever there were vacancies to fill, an announcement would appear in the Viennese newspapers.   Then all the boys who had good voices, and were sufficiently trained in music, would come for the auditions, hoping to be admitted to the choir and gain the coveted scholarships.

On this morning of September 30th, 1808, there were quite a number of contestants in the Konvikt Music Room.   The Choir had advertised for only two singers, so Franz knew that most of the boys would be disappointed; he sent up a little prayer that he might be one of the lucky ones.

After the preliminary questions, Herr Lang came to the important business of the examinations.

"What are your musical qualifications?" he asked Franz, looking at him severely over his spectacles.

The child began to lose a little of his shyness. "I have studied singing and harmony, sir, under Herr Michael Holzer, organist of the Lichtenthal church." (What could have happened to Herr Holzer? Franz wondered.   He had promised to be there for the auditions, but perhaps the old organist had forgotten, or had stayed too late at the tavern the night before. . . . Franz felt lonely and forsaken in the midst of all these strangers.)

Director Lang turned to the man who sat beside him on the platform. For the first time Franz noticed the extraordinary person who had the seat of honor among the judges. He was a thin, elegantly dressed little man, with a large wart on one side of his nose. His swarthy complexion and arrogant manner marked him as a foreigner.

"That must be the great Salieri!" thought Franz with a start of excitement. He had often heard of this famous Italian, who was one of the most celebrated musicians in Vienna and Chief Music-director, or "Kapellmeister", of the Royal Austrian Court. Next to Signor Salieri on the judges' platform sat Wendel Ruziczka, director of music at the Konvikt School.

"This boy comes very well recommended," Herr Lang said in an aside, handing the Kapellmeister a letter.

With a graceful gesture Salieri took a pinch of snuff from a jewel-studded snuffbox, and then glanced casually through the letter.

"You say you can sing?" he said to Franz with a strong Italian accent. "*Bene*—but that is not enough. Can you play—ah—instruments of music?"

Young Schubert was so fascinated by the Italian's long, thin hands, and the elegant snuffbox, that he hardly heard the question. Then he suddenly realized that he had not answered.

"No, Your Excellency—I mean *yes*, Your Excellency. I—I can play the piano, and the violin . . ." he drew a deep breath, "and the viola."

"Very well," the Kapellmeister said. "Let us hear you. We shall—ah—judge of your ability."

First came the singing tests. Franz was paralyzed with terror, but as he opened his mouth to sing, he heard a sound at the door and caught a glimpse out of the corner of his eye of a familiar stout, gray-haired figure just entering the room. It was old Michael Holzer—he hadn't forgotten after all! Young Schubert knew that his teacher was expecting him to win high honors. The boy made up his mind that he wouldn't disappoint him. . . . He squared his shoulders, and his clear, soprano voice rang fearlessly through the Music Room.

When he had finished singing it was plain to be seen that the judges were impressed, and after he had shown his ability on the piano, violin, and viola they were still more so.

To complete the examinations Franz had to go through a number of tests in sight-reading, transposing music, and writing it down from dictation. At the conclusion, the judges whispered among themselves in excitement, and there was quite a stir throughout the room. Nothing, however, was announced until all the candidates had been heard.

At the close of the long session, Herr Direktor Lang stood up and cleared his throat impressively.

"First honors," he announced, "go to a boy who has shown outstanding musical talent. The judges consider him exceptional."

Franz, shivering in his seat with excitement, wondered if he dared to hope. . . .

"Franz Peter Seraph Schubert," Herr Lang continued solemnly, "you are admitted to the Imperial Choir of Vienna *cum laude*, and it gives me pleasure to present you with a scholarship to the Konvikt School."

Franz was in such a daze that the boys sitting beside him had to nudge him vigorously to make him stand up and acknowledge the honor.

At the close of the session Herr Holzer congratulated his pupil with tears in his eyes. "I knew you would cause a sensation!" he said proudly. "But, best of all, perhaps now your Herr Papa will see that music really counts for something!"

Franz was immediately installed as a pupil in the Imperial Konvikt School.

When he went down for dinner he found a very different attitude among the boys. Instead of the teasing condescension with which they had greeted him earlier that same morning, there was now something very like respect in the way they looked at the mild-mannered, bespectacled new student.

Holzapfel made a place for Franz beside him at the long table. Director Lang sat at the head, and opposite him—nearest to Franz—was Prefect Walch, a thin, sandy-haired man with a long nose and sharp eyes who kept a close watch on the students' behavior.

"Rotten food here," Holzapfel remarked amiably out of the side of his mouth, when Prefect Walch was looking in another direction.

Franz was too shy to answer, but he nodded and smiled in such a friendly way that "Wooden-Apple" decided he was going to like this new boy. "Hope your family will send you 'hand-me-outs' from home. If not, you'll probably starve. . . ."

"Silence!" called the Prefect severely. "You know it is forbidden to talk during meals."

Franz, who was accustomed to much lively conversation at his own family table, felt suddenly very homesick. Life was frugal enough in the Schubert household; but it was nothing to the Spartan existence he was to find at the Konvikt. Here the meals were poorly cooked and insufficient; the boys had to rise before daybreak and dress in damp, unheated dormitories that were like ice in the winter; then they were obliged to attend prayers before breakfast, and again in the evening. Every minute of the day was taken up with studies and other duties, and the only free time allowed was a short period before supper. On Sunday, following the church service, the boys could return to their homes for the remainder of the day.

Holzapfel took Franz under his special care. After that first noon meal they went upstairs together to the room where the new student was to be fitted to a school uniform. This consisted of light-colored knee breeches with buckles, a long waistcoat and a white stock, and an open-breasted dark-brown coat with a gold epaulet over the left shoulder. A flat, three-cornered hat completed the costume. Franz felt very grand when he finally exchanged his shabby smock for this fine suit.

As they went down the stairs, Holzapfel said admiringly: "You're awfully good at music, aren't you! Even old Salieri was impressed this morning. You'll have to play in the school orchestra, you know."

"I hope I can!" Franz replied with enthusiasm. "I have always wanted to play in an orchestra."

They were just passing by the room where the auditions had been held. "We practise in here every

evening," his companion continued. "I play the
'cello," he added modestly.

Franz looked through the open door. "Are the
students allowed to go in there?" he asked eagerly.
"Can they use the piano?"

"Well—" Holzapfel answered, "I suppose the
Herr Direktor wouldn't mind. But no one ever has
time to bother with music outside of school hours, and
besides, it is always so gruesomely cold in the Music
Room . . ."

Franz's eyes brightened. Perhaps he could have
the room all to himself, and a *piano!*—a place where
he could write music undisturbed. What did he care
if it was cold! Music would warm his heart—and
his fingers, too.

Late that afternoon, when the recreation bell
finally rang, Franz left the boys to their noisy games,
and went quietly up to the Music Room.

It was cold and deserted, and almost dark. He
listened a moment; no one seemed to be around that
part of the building. He tiptoed in, and with beating
heart lifted the cover of the piano. Did he dare . . . ?

From one pocket Franz drew out a stump of a
candle, lit it, and placed it on the piano. From the
other he pulled a crumpled piece of paper and spread
it on the music-rack. Very softly, the notes at first
scarcely sounding, he played the little melody he had
written that morning.

Now he forgot his homesickness. He felt suddenly light-hearted and gay. The cold, bleak Konvikt building was transformed into a palace of beautiful sounds—sounds that he himself brought forth from within his own heart.

Franz, absorbed in what he loved best, was completely happy.

CHAPTER II

Father Schubert

FRANZ'S earliest memories centered in his father's school in the Lichtenthal district. The elder Schubert had come to Vienna when he was a penniless boy of eighteen, beginning his career as a schoolteacher's assistant.

After several years of grinding toil he was promoted to the position of headmaster in the Lichtenthal seminary, and he thought that his fortune was made. He did not realize what a hard struggle lay ahead of him. His wages were so small that he could never, even with the strictest economies, make both ends meet.

Yet in spite of his poverty, when he was twenty Franz Theodor married a young woman named Elisabet Vietz, who was cook in the household of a wealthy

Austrian nobleman.   Although she was seven years
his senior, schoolmaster Schubert felt sure that she
would make a quiet, capable wife.

"I cannot afford to give you much of a home,
Elisabet," he told her, "and certainly none of the
luxuries."

"I do not mind," she replied gravely.   "Am I
not used to hard work?"

They started their life together in a small house
called *Zum Rothen Krebsen*.   Conditions were very
primitive at "The Red Crab"; there were none of
the "necessities" which we think indispensable.   In
those days only the finest homes in Vienna could
boast even such an ordinary convenience as running
water, and the poorer people did not dream of such
a luxury.

Elisabet carried in large pails from the fountain
in the courtyard outside, and never complained when
the wood-stove smoked, or the meager supply of tallow candles ran out and there was no money with
which to buy more.   Nor did she think of grumbling
over the thousand and one inconveniences and economies which were a commonplace in the Schubert
household.

In addition to all these hardships, each year
Elisabet brought another child into the world.   First
came Ignatz, who was like a small edition of his
father—steady, unimaginative, and dependable.

"He shall be a schoolmaster, Elisabet!" the young father insisted proudly. His wife, who thought less highly of the profession (at least from a material standpoint!), said nothing.

Following Ignatz, eight more children were born, all of whom died in infancy. Each year Father Schubert made another entry on the flyleaf of the large Bible, under the heading: "Births and deaths in the family of Schoolteacher Franz Schubert". And each time he would remark, with mournful resignation: "It is the will of God! If these little ones had lived, Heaven knows how we should have managed to take care of them."

When Ignatz was ten years old, a second son finally survived the sad procession. They named him Ferdinand, and two years later a third boy, Karl, came to join the family.

With three children to support, Father Schubert was at his wits' end. By now the Lichtenthal school had grown into a prosperous and well-attended institution; but his salary was no larger than before. He had spent all of his father's small legacy, and was obliged to borrow from the money-lenders to help pay the rent and buy food. He finally petitioned the *Landesregierung* to give him a better post; but the Government authorities refused to consider the application.

Herr Schubert was in despair. For Elisabet had

just informed him that another baby was on the way.
This was her twelfth child, and the next to the last.

Franz Peter Seraph Schubert was born on January 30th, 1797, shortly before the nineteenth century
opened.   At that date, Mozart had been dead for six
years, young Beethoven was 27, and Haydn—still
active—was a man of 65.

There was no rejoicing over Franz's birth; on
the contrary, poor Elisabet, weighed down with the
cares of her household and broken in health from
many years of childbearing, could only sigh as she
looked at the new baby in her arms, while Father
Schubert prayed that he would be able to provide
enough food to keep this son alive.

Little Franz had every reason to be serious and
sober-hearted.   But although there was such bitter
poverty in the household, and both his father and his
mother were serious and careworn, he was born with
an exceptionally sunny and contented disposition.   As
a baby he rarely cried; he would lie for hours in his
wooden cradle, absorbed in thoughts of his own that
made him smile with a quiet, inner joy.   If his
mother found time to sit beside him with her mending basket, rocking the cradle with one foot and hum-

ming some old German lullaby in her tuneless voice, he would laugh and crow with delight.

Frau Schubert was not musical, although she enjoyed listening to others. But her husband, like most of the Viennese of that time, made music as a matter of course. He played the 'cello and violin, and gave lessons to each of his sons in succession.

Vienna, during the latter part of the eighteenth century, was known throughout Europe for its devotion to music. All the leading composers of the time were attracted to the gay city on the Danube. Here "Papa Haydn" wrote symphonies for the private orchestra of Prince Esterházy, and the young Mozart composed operas that stirred the people of Vienna to a frenzy of enthusiasm. Later came the mighty Beethoven, and there were scores of others less important.

Even the common people shared the general enthusiasm. There was music in every household; family groups played together and were often joined by friends. There were no moving-pictures nor automobiles in those days, and music was the chief recreation of the people.

Herr Schubert had quite a number of friends who came in to play chamber music with him in the little house called "The Red Crab". Prominent among these was Michael Holzer, organist of the Lichtenthal church.

Franz from his earliest days was fascinated by any kind of music. When Father Schubert tuned up his 'cello, the boy would run to his favorite corner and sit there quietly to listen. If Frau Elisabet said it was too late and he must go to bed, little Franz would beg to have the door left open, so he could hear the playing.

Herr Schubert was amused at his son's passion for beautiful sounds. Music to him was an agreeable pastime, but not to be taken too seriously. He was much more concerned over Franz's apparent indifference to the lessons in reading and writing which he tried to give him. The boy could not seem to learn; he would pucker up his forehead, stare stupidly at the page, and finally burst into tears.

Michael Holzer witnessed one of these scenes on a visit to the Schuberts'. He watched the child attentively, then drew the father to one side. "There is something wrong here," he said thoughtfully. "Franz is not really unintelligent, and he is usually a good, obedient boy. Perhaps he doesn't see so well as he should."

When Father Schubert took his son to an optician, it was discovered that the child had very weak and nearsighted eyes. After he was fitted to glasses —clumsy, steel-rimmed spectacles which he was to wear and depend on for the rest of his days—Franz learned so rapidly that his father became prouder of him than of any of his other sons.

At the time Franz Schubert came into the world, Vienna was one of the largest and finest cities in Europe; but it had changed very little since the Middle Ages. The old fortified walls still surrounded the main part of the town, and there was the same contrast between fine Gothic architecture and disreputable, unsanitary hovels, narrow, dirty streets and broad central squares that had existed for several hundred years. It was not until nearly a century later that the walls were torn down, and the broad, leafy "Ring" Avenue* took their place.

In the center of the city, flanked by a large open square, stood the magnificent old cathedral of St. Stephen. Streets radiated out from this point in every direction, but only one, the *Graben*, was paved; the others were narrow and dark, and little more than mud-holes when it rained. The people who lived on either side of these streets were obliged to bank up the earth in front of their doors to keep the mud out of their houses.

* So named because it surrounds the city like a ring.

To go on foot through the streets was a dangerous undertaking. At any moment some wealthy nobleman's carriage might come rushing by, attended by one or more footmen running beside it, and woe to the pedestrians who did not get out of the way fast enough. At night there were thugs and pickpockets lurking in the doorways, and no one went out alone after dark unless on urgent business.

The rulers of the Austrian Empire were harsh masters who imposed heavy taxes and restrictions on the people. They had spies everywhere—a kind of secret police called the *Naderer*, who would report a person on the slightest suspicion. As a result, innocent citizens were frequently arrested and sent away to hard labor.

There were constant wars; everyone lived in terror of conscription, for few of the soldiers returned from the long and bloody campaigns, and those that did were usually broken in body and health.

But in spite of all these afflictions, the Viennese people were by nature so gay and pleasure-loving that they managed to lead a fairly happy existence. The taverns and coffee-houses were always filled with jolly crowds, eating and drinking as if they had no care in the world; and on holidays it was the custom to go out into the woods surrounding the city, to dance and make merry.

On the edge of the Lichtenthal district stretched

the Wienerwald, one of Vienna's most beautiful forests. On Sundays, when the weather was fine, Frau Schubert often put up a basket of lunch and went with her family to spend the day in the woods.

Father Schubert usually had some lesson-papers to correct; Ignatz would stretch out under a tree with a book, while Ferdinand and Karl amused themselves by building dams over the streams. But little Franz had a way of wandering off by himself. He loved to listen to the sounds of the forest—the wind in the trees, the murmuring brook, the hum of insects, and the songs of the birds.

Usually there would be other holiday crowds in the Wienerwald, and then, Franz had learned from experience, there was sure to be singing and dancing, and perhaps someone playing on a fiddle or flute. At these times a small chubby figure with solemn, bespectacled eyes would draw closer and closer to the revelers. Music drew Franz like a magnet; he would forget his natural shyness in his desire to hear the gay tunes.

One day the Schuberts' youngest son disappeared completely. The whole family searched for him in a panic, scattering in every direction through the forest. At last they came upon a band of gypsies dancing under the green oak trees to the mad music of a temperamental violinist. Faster and faster whirled the gypsies, bright-colored skirts and scarfs flying. Wilder and wilder grew the music.

There, on the step of a gaily painted covered wagon, they found Franz. He was so enthralled by the fascinating new music that he could hardly be persuaded to come home with them.

The dancing of the gypsies and the rhythms of their wild music made a lasting impression on the child. This was strengthened in later years by a trip to Hungary and, combined with his natural Viennese heritage of love for the dance, was responsible for some of Schubert's loveliest music in later years.

When Franz was three years old, his mother's father—a locksmith in Silesia—died and left her a small inheritance.

It seemed like a fortune to the struggling schoolmaster and his wife. After much discussion they decided to buy the house in Lichtenthal where the school's classes were held.

"At least we will be sure of a roof over our heads, and you will not have to walk back and forth to your classes every day," said Elisabet with her usual quiet wisdom.

The house seemed very spacious when they first

moved in. But before long it grew crowded almost beyond endurance. There were now over two hundred pupils in each day's classes, and even the family had hardly enough room for their needs. A fourteenth child (the fifth and last to survive) was born in 1801, and the Schuberts named her Theresa.

Father Schubert was busy with his school duties all during the day, but he still found time to give music lessons to his sons. Ignatz, soon to become an assistant to his father in the school, played both piano and violin.

Next in line was Ferdinand. He was not much interested in music, but his father insisted that he must learn to play the violin. Franz, although three years younger ("much too young to be taught music", his father insisted), would listen to the lessons with absorbed interest. He begged Ferdinand to let him try his violin.

"Wait until you are older," his brother told him with lofty superiority. "Violins are not for babies. You might drop it. . . ."

One day, however, when Ferdinand and Karl had gone on an errand for their mother, Franz stole up into the room which he shared with his brothers, and took the coveted violin out of its case. With painstaking care (*certainly* he would not drop it!) he placed the instrument tightly under his chin and tried to make his fingers and the bow move in the way he had seen his father teach Ferdinand.

At first he felt very awkward. The sounds he made were so dreadful that they hurt his ears; but presently the playing went better, and before long he was doing his brother's exercises with scarcely any difficulty.

Suddenly there were steps outside the door. Franz, in a panic, tried to hide the violin.

"That is excellent, Ferdinand!" he heard his father say in a pleased voice. "I did not know you could play so— Bless my soul!" Herr Schubert cried as he opened the door and discovered Franz. "Don't tell me that was *you* playing just now!"

When Father Schubert, now convinced that Franz *was* old enough, began to give the boy lessons on the violin, he was amazed at the rapidity with which his youngest son learned. It was only necessary to indicate how a thing should be done—almost at once Franz played it perfectly, as if he knew instinctively without being taught. Ignatz gave his brother piano lessons, and was equally surprised at the child's extraordinary facility. Herr Holzer soon heard of Franz's talent.

Michael Holzer was a stout, genial soul with red nose and graying hair, and he knew more about music than many of the best professors in Vienna. If he had not been so fond of his beer and *Schnapps*, he might have risen to considerable importance in the musical world of the city. But Herr Holzer was indolent and easy-going; the years went by, and he was content to remain choirmaster and organist of the Lichtenthal church.

"What did I tell you!" he cried when he heard Franz play. "Have I not always said the boy had a natural talent for music? Mark my words—he will be a great musician one of these days."

Father Schubert threw up his hands. "What are you saying, Michael? A *musician?* Heaven forbid! It is hard enough to make a living as a schoolmaster, but a musician. . . . Now what, I ask, would *you* do if you had a wife and family to support?"

Herr Holzer grumbled a little under his breath about some things' being worth more than money, but he didn't argue the question with his friend. Later he drew Franz to one side. "Would you like to come up to the organ loft some afternoon, while I go over the Sunday cantata?"

Franz had never seen the mighty instrument at close hand, and he was enchanted at the prospect.

"Come then, tomorrow at five," the old organist whispered as he left.

The sun had already set when Franz entered the church the following afternoon. Inside, the shadows were fast deepening, and he thought the stained-glass windows were even lovelier than in the bright morning light of the Sunday services.

As he opened the door to the tower staircase that led to the organ loft, a sudden burst of music came from above. Franz felt his way up the dark stairs, and in a moment was standing beside Herr Holzer at the organ. He watched in wonder as the old man's agile fingers played first on one keyboard and then on another, while at the same time he used both feet on the pedals below.

"So!" Herr Holzer exclaimed as the last note of the Bach cantata faded away in the empty church. "Did you like it?"

Franz was too filled with emotion to speak. He could only nod his head in a dumb, ecstatic way.

"Perhaps *you* would like to learn to play the organ?" the old musician continued, as nonchalantly as if he were suggesting that they take a walk together.

This time Franz found his voice. "*Aber, Herr Holzer*—do you really think I could learn?"

The organist nodded his head gravely. He lighted a candle on the keyboard beside his music. "Of course you can!"

To himself he added: "Michael Holzer knows

a musician when he sees one! And no one—not even the Devil himself—can blow out the divine spark when it is once lit."

Aloud he said to the boy: "That isn't all; you must have lessons in singing, in composition, harmony, counterpoint. . . ."

The light from the candle shone on the boy's spectacles; but it was nothing to the light in Franz's eyes. Then suddenly it died down as quickly as it had come.

"But, my father—" he began. "Do you think Father would allow me?"

"Never mind!" Herr Holzer exclaimed. "I will take care of *him*."

Years later Herr Schubert, in writing of his illustrious son's early career, said: "When he was eight I grounded him in violin playing. . . . Then I sent him for singing lessons to Michael Holzer, choirmaster in Lichtenthal. This teacher used to assure me with tears in his eyes that he had never had such a pupil before: 'When I begin to teach him something new, I find that he knows it already,' he said. 'So I have given up teaching him anything, and simply listen to him in amazed silence.'"

Ignatz, who gave Franz his first piano lessons, wrote: "To my astonishment he came to me after a few months and said he required no further instruction, as he would teach himself in the future. And indeed he was so far advanced, even in that short time, that I had to acknowledge him my superior, whom I should have difficulty in overtaking."

It was many years, however, before Father Schubert was willing to admit the genius of his son Franz. Meanwhile other and more pressing matters claimed his attention, and it was largely because of this that he allowed the boy to continue his studies with Herr Holzer.

As Franz grew older, Herr Schubert became seriously concerned over his youngest son's education. To be a schoolmaster (and Father Schubert hoped that all his boys would follow this profession) required even for the lower grades a special certificate of learning. Franz's father did not see how he could possibly afford to send his youngest son to the proper schools.

Then one day in September 1808 Herr Holzer came puffing into the Schuberts' dining-room just as they were finishing their noon meal. In one hand he waved the *Wiener Zeitung*, Vienna's leading newspaper.

"Have you seen this?" he asked breathlessly. "Here is the answer to your problem."

"What do you mean?" demanded Father Schubert.

"Well—you want Franz to have an education at the University, don't you?   And first he must go to a preparatory school."

"Yes," said the schoolmaster in a puzzled voice. "But you know I cannot afford to send him there."

"That's just it!" Herr Holzer exclaimed triumphantly.   "If Franz could get into the Imperial Chapel Choir they would give him a scholarship to the Konvikt School, and"—he pointed to an announcement in the newspaper—"they have just advertised that two places are vacant."

"Do you think Franz has a chance of getting one of them?" Herr Schubert asked, interested but a little doubtful, for he knew how difficult it was to gain admittance to the Imperial Choir.

"I'll stake my life on it!" his friend replied.

CHAPTER III

At the Sign of the Black Horse

ON Franz's first Sunday morning following his entrance into the Konvikt, Frau Schubert was just opening the upstairs window to water her geraniums when she saw a familiar small figure trudging towards the house.

"Franzl!" she called. "Is that *you?*"

Her son looked up with a chuckle of delight. "*Aber ja, liebes Mühmchen,* coming as fast as I can!" He broke into a run and reached the front door just as his mother threw it open to welcome him.

On weekdays there was a constant hum of activity in the house on the "Gate of Heaven Street"

(*Himmelpfortgrund*). Crowds of children filled the
small, low-ceilinged rooms and were taught their lessons by schoolmaster Schubert and his assistants. But
on Sundays the place wore an entirely different air;
for Sunday was "family day", and the Schuberts forgot lessons to enjoy themselves in rest and merrymaking.

Franz could hardly wait to get home—he had
so much to tell about the school, and his new life,
and his friends. The long walk back to Lichtenthal
seemed endless; but finally in the distance he saw the
familiar sign of the dashing black horse over his
father's door.

Most of the houses in Vienna at that time were
known by name rather than by number. Painted
signs hung before the doors, some of them real works
of art done by the best painters of the day. Franz
still remembered the picture of the large red crab on
the house where he was born. His father's present
home was called "The Black Horse" (*Zum
Schwarzen Rössl*).

Just at this moment "The Black Horse" was
having an unexpected shower bath from Frau Schubert's forgotten watering-pot above. Franz laughingly dodged the stream of water and threw his arms
around his mother's neck.

He did not notice how tired she looked. But
then, no one ever noticed Frau Schubert much at any

time, she was so quiet and reserved and had so little to say. Her own family hardly realized how much they depended on her untiring toil and loving care.

Because Elisabet had been a cook before her marriage, she always felt herself on a lower social level than her schoolmaster husband; so she remained content to spend her time in cooking and cleaning and in caring for her children and household. When Herr Schubert's brilliant friends came to visit him, she would retire to her kitchen, or else sit quietly in a corner with the large basket of mending that was never empty.

"Well, my son," Father Schubert said as Franz came in, "we heard from Herr Holzer of your success in the examinations." He put his hand on the boy's shoulder and looked at him gravely. "I am pleased that you did so well. And now I hope that you will take advantage of your opportunities and not spend too much time on music."

Franz remembered the new tune in his pocket and felt suddenly guilty. It was a good tune—he had hoped to show it to his father; but now he thought better of this idea. Perhaps he would let his brother Ferdinand see what he had written, or maybe Karl?

There was a delicious smell of sauerkraut and roasting apples through the house. In the dining-room, which was also the family living-room, the

sunlight streamed through latticed windows and lit
up the polished surface of Frau Schubert's special
pride and joy: a huge old carved sideboard which had
belonged to her father.   The sun shone too on the
tiles of the big porcelain stove in the corner, and made
Tyl-Tyl, the canary, sing loudly in his wicker cage.
Franz was so happy to be back in these beloved surroundings that he wanted to sing, too.

Seven-year-old Theresa, the baby of the family,
was kneeling on the floor beside Karl, who was drawing a picture; Ferdinand was sitting by the window,
deep in a book, but when Franz came in they all
jumped to their feet and crowded around him with
eager questions.

"How do you like the Konvikt?" asked Ferdinand.   He was a serious boy of fourteen, and Franz
liked him best of his three brothers.

"Do they have games—do they teach you drawing?" queried Karl all in one breath.

"What is a *Konvikt*, Franzl?" Theresa cried,
pulling him by the sleeve to get his attention.

He was laughingly trying to answer all their
questions at once when Ignatz, the eldest of the family, came in.

Ignatz was now a young man of twenty-one, and
had been his father's assistant for several years already—stolid, conscientious, and hard-working.   His
whole life was bounded by the walls of the school-

room, and while he had very little imagination, he did well whatever he undertook, whether it was teaching the children in his father's school or playing the violin in the family quartet.

Franz had to start at the beginning and tell everything that had happened to him since he entered the Konvikt. But he did not mention the hours he had spent in the Music Room, playing softly on the old piano, or writing down bits of music on scraps of paper that he ruled himself.

In the midst of his recital Herr Holzer arrived. Father Schubert had invited Franz's old music-teacher to have dinner with them, and for once he arrived entirely—or *almost* entirely—sober.

"*You* showed the judges, my lad!" Holzer exclaimed with a resounding whack on Franz's shoulder that nearly knocked the boy off his feet. "I knew you would—I knew you'd strike them dumb!!" He shook all over with laughter, and his ruddy cheeks grew even redder.

Herr Holzer always looked as if he were about to burst the seams of his clothes; no one could put down more steins of beer in an evening than Michael Holzer, and everyone knows what beer will do to the figure. . . . When he laughed—which was most of the time—Franz waited in fearful fascination for the expected pop.

"*Bitte zu Tisch!*" called Frau Schubert from

the kitchen. "Will the *Herrschaften* please be seated for dinner."

They needed no second invitation. "It is always an 'occasion' to eat at your table, Frau Elisabet," Herr Holzer called genially.

Father Schubert looked pleased. "You speak true, friend Michael," he exclaimed. "My Elisabet is a remarkable cook. Even"—his eyes clouded over —"when there is scanty fare to do with she manages to make something tasty for the table."

"We don't get good things like this at school," Franz said, smacking his lips in anticipation. "*Was gibt es, Mütterchen?* What shall we have today?"

"Oh, a feast!" answered Karl jubilantly. "Only think—rich bean soup, red cabbage sauerkraut, potatoes, and—" he paused a moment to make it more dramatic—"a pot-roast of beef!"

Herr Holzer sighed ecstatically, and all the children beamed. It was not every day that meat graced the Schuberts' table.

"And *Apfelstrudel* besides," cried little Theresa, not to be outdone in surprises.

Father Schubert shook his head gravely. "What luxury! And what a contrast, eh, friend Michael, to three years ago?"

Everyone at the table grew suddenly quiet. They had not forgotten the terrible privations following Napoleon's occupation of Vienna in 1805. The soldiers had pillaged the whole city, and there was so little food left that many of the poor died of starvation.

"Yes," Herr Schubert continued, "if I hadn't been appointed assessor to the Association for Schoolmasters' Widows we should probably have starved at that time."

"You should have had that appointment long before," Herr Holzer remarked between loud mouthfuls of bean soup.

The schoolmaster sighed. "Four times I asked to be transferred to a better position, and each time the Government refused my petition. 'Teachers must be stoics,' they said. Imagine that! 'Teachers must be willing to submit to any privation for the privilege of dedicating their lives to the young. . . .'" A note of bitterness crept into Herr Schubert's voice. "*Stoics!*" he repeated. "All very well for the teachers—but what of their families?"

Frau Schubert, at the other end of the table, gave her husband an understanding smile, but his friend rapped sharply on the table with his great fist.

"You were too easy!" he said in a loud voice. "Too efficient. Why,"—even the soup was forgotten in his indignation—"didn't *you* take this Lichtenthal school when there was hardly a pupil in it, when no one else would have it, and build it up to one of the finest institutions in the community?"

"The Government knows very well what Father has done," Ignatz broke in ponderously. "Do you remember what they said when he was appointed Assessor?"

Frau Schubert spoke unexpectedly: "They said," she quoted, " 'Not only is Herr Schubert a man of excellent character and absolute integrity, but also—though he is bound to instruct only twenty poor children gratuitously in the school—he has voluntarily taken forty from various parishes; and, because his excellent method of teaching is generally known, his school is frequently attended by pupils from more distant suburbs, so that they cannot find accommodation even in the several rooms of his house.' "

"Bravo! Frau Elisabet," said Holzer, applauding vigorously, "I can add to that. . . ."

Herr Schubert, who was secretly pleased but would not have had anyone suspect it, tried to stop his friend. "Please, please!" he cried.

Herr Holzer refused to be silenced. "Didn't the Archbishop himself praise you? I saw the letter he wrote, and I can remember most of it: 'On account of Herr Schubert's gentle character, kind treatment of the children, peaceable conduct towards all people, his sober and orderly Christian life, and his untiring fulfillment of his duties as a teacher, he has gained the love and confidence not only of the young, but also of his own and other parish communities to such an extent that he has increased the number of his pupils from a few to over three hundred'!" He stopped for breath.

Father Schubert's eyes were moist. "I don't deserve all that," he said simply. His eyes traveled around the table and rested first on Ignatz, solid, dependable, on Ferdinand, following close in his brother's footsteps, on little Theresa and on Karl, and lastly on the round bespectacled face of his youngest son.

"I only ask that I may give my children all they need, and that they in return shall be God-fearing and a credit to their family," he said solemnly.

Franz, his heart filled with love for his hardworking parent, thought to himself, "Some day I shall make you proud of *me!*"

When dinner was over and the dishes had been cleared away from the table, Karl told Franz to follow him. He took his brother up to the attic bedroom that he shared with Ferdinand, and reaching under his pillow on the large double bed, pulled out his beloved sketch-book.

"Look, Franzl! I found some paints at school —one of the boys had thrown them away, they weren't much good—but I made a picture."

Franz recognized the *Himmelpfortgrund* with a lurid sun setting over "The Black Horse". "But it is very good, Karl," he said with genuine admiration, "especially the horse. Why, you could easily be a sign-painter."

Karl clasped his hands together and gave a sigh. "I should give anything to be a painter. But Father would never consent to it."

Franz nodded gravely. "Yes, I know—he thinks we should all be schoolteachers, like Ignatz." He looked out of the window with a thoughtful frown. "I think it's stupid, teaching silly children. Music is much more wonderful." He pulled out a paper from his pocket. "See what a lovely tune I've written here. . . ."

"Karl—Franz! Are you in here?" The door opened suddenly and Father Schubert came in. "We are ready to start playing now—" He stopped short as he saw the guilty expressions on the boys' faces. "What have you there?" He went over to Franz and took the paper from him.

"Music! Hum-m-m, Franz, I must talk to you seriously. Karl, go down to the dining-room and tell the others we will be there in a minute."

As Karl went out, with a sympathetic glance at his brother's disconsolate face, Father Schubert sat down on the bed.

"When did you write this?"

Franz blushed and stammered, but he was too honest to lie to his father. "Last week, sir, at the Konvikt," he replied.

"My son, I know your passion for music. I can even understand it because I like music, too. Don't we all play together and go to hear the concerts in Herr Holzer's church?"

"But, Father—" Franz began timidly.

"I know, I know," Herr Schubert interrupted. "But it isn't as if you had no music at the Konvikt; there will be plenty of it with all the church services and the school orchestra and lessons. All I ask is, don't waste your time trying to compose. In the first place, you know I can't afford to buy you music-paper. . . ."

"Oh, but I can rule my own!" Franz cried.

"Yes," said his father with a frown, "you have done that before, but *any* paper costs money, and you know how we have to watch every penny." Herr Schubert sighed. "I wonder if you realize what a struggle we have had just to keep you children fed and clothed! Well, the others are waiting for us to come down and play with them, but don't forget, Franz, studies must come before music!"

Franz was only too glad to get out his viola and join the family quartet. Father Schubert played the 'cello (rather badly, Franz secretly thought), Ignatz was first violinist, and Ferdinand had the second fiddle part. Today their group was augmented by Herr Holzer and by Karl, who was learning, during Franz's absence, to play the viola.

"I have brought a new quartet today," said Herr Holzer, pulling a rolled-up manuscript from the tails of his voluminous frock-coat. "It is by that young composer everyone is talking about, Ludwig van Beethoven." He drew out a pair of horn-rimmed spectacles, adjusted them carefully over his red nose, and peered at the score. "Dedicated to Count Rasumovsky."

"I don't think much of Herr van Beethoven's music," Father Schubert exclaimed. "He is too modern—too daring in his harmonies. But let us try it."

Franz was more interested. He had been to a concert the year before, when Beethoven had played one of his own concertos with the Vienna Philharmonic Orchestra. Franz remembered how the celebrated musician had lost himself in the music, throwing his shaggy head about and playing as if nothing else in the world had any importance. Franz understood. . . . When he himself played—and even more, when he wrote down the music that was always running through his head—he too forgot the world and his surroundings.

As they plunged into the Beethoven quartet, Franz thought of the new tune he had composed that week. Perhaps he could make it into a string quartet! On and on the Schuberts, father and sons, and Herr Holzer played; then suddenly Father Schubert stopped his playing and looked at the clock. "*Himmel!* Where has the time gone? Franz, you must start back immediately—and hurry, too, or you will be late."

Franz put away his viola and hastened to kiss his mother and little Theresa good-bye. As he went out of the door Ferdinand waylaid him and slipped a little package into his hand. "I saved my *Apfelstrudel* for you, little brother," he whispered.

Franz, who dearly loved good things to eat, was filled with emotion. It was very hard to leave all these dear ones and go back alone to the cold, gloomy Konvikt. But then he remembered the Music Room, and he thought again of his gay little tune. What a good chance he would have, on the long walk back, to work out in his mind the different parts for a string quartet!

CHAPTER IV

Music Comes First

"NOW, now, young gentlemen," Herr Ruziczka cried as the Konvikt orchestra
tuned up. "A little less noise, please!"
Every evening after supper the boys
played for an hour in the Music Room. First there
was usually an overture, then came a symphony by
Mozart, Haydn, or Beethoven, and to finish, another
overture.

The Konvikt, with its special training for the
singers of the Vienna Imperial Chapel Choir, was an
outgrowth of the old ecclesiastical Singing Schools
of previous centuries. In the Middle Ages music had

been almost entirely confined to the Church; the religious training of the choristers was considered more important than their musical instruction. Gradually, as music came to have a more important place, the Singing Schools devoted less time to religious matters and more to the teaching of music. The Konvikt, although it had a full curriculum of regular studies, was really the forerunner of our modern music conservatories.

Here the boys of the Imperial Choir received a thorough grounding in music, and were also required to take part in the school orchestra. Since the choristers were all good musicians (none but the best were admitted to the choir), this young orchestra enjoyed quite a reputation in Vienna. On warm evenings, when the windows were left open, crowds would gather in the square outside to listen to its playing.

There was a great deal of confusion in the Music Room on Franz's first evening at the Konvikt. The tallow candles on each music-stand were half burned down—some even ready to gutter out. No one seemed to have the right music; the violin parts were mixed up with the 'cello parts, and the oboe with the clarinet. Herr Ruziczka, the ruffles of his shirt all in disorder, rushed from one group to another, trying to get things straightened out. He was muttering to himself all the while, when suddenly his eyes fell on Franz, who stood at the end of the room looking on with eager curiosity.

"*You* there!" he called. "Aren't you the new boy who did so well at the examinations?"

All eyes were turned to the newcomer, and Franz was so embarrassed that he blushed a fiery red.

"Come here and help me straighten things out," the conductor demanded. "I don't know why it is I have so much trouble getting someone to look after the music and stands. Just a few minutes' work, but no one can find time to do it."

Franz was quite in his element. He always took care of the family quartet music at home, and his schoolmaster father had trained him to be neat and orderly in all his ways. "I shall be glad to take care of it for you, sir," he said. In a short time order was restored.

"Take your place in the second stand of the violins," Herr Ruziczka told Franz. "I will try you out there."

Franz did not find any music at his place, so he stood up and read over the shoulder of the first violinist, who sat just in front of him. He noticed that this was the older boy who had come to his rescue the morning of his arrival. Gradually a few familiar faces began to stand out; he could see "Wooden-Apple" sawing away in the 'cello section; Franz Eckel, tall and thin, played the bassoon, puffing out his cheeks and growing quite red in the face; and Stadler's round figure matched his kettledrums.

Young Schubert was terribly excited, though no

one would have suspected it from his quiet appearance. He had always wanted to hear wood winds, drums, and brasses at close hand. The strings he knew well—violin, viola, and even the 'cello and double-bass. But he was anxious to know more about the other instruments in the orchestra.

Herr Ruziczka tapped sharply with his baton. "We will begin with Mozart's Overture to *The Marriage of Figaro*," he announced.

Franz loved Mozart best of all composers, and this overture was his favorite. He tucked his violin under his chin, and in a moment forgot everything but the music. It was a new experience for him to play in such a large group—as part of one great whole. His own limited tones were now augmented by all the others into a richness of sound that filled him with an exhilarating sense of power. He felt lifted beyond his own individual capacities.

As the Overture came to a close, the first violinist turned and looked at Franz in surprise. Josef Spaun, a tall, aristocratic-looking youth of twenty, was not a student of the Konvikt. He boarded there and attended the University across the street, but his interest in music and excellence as a violinist made him invaluable in the school orchestra.

Describing the scene in later years, Spaun—who was to become Schubert's closest friend at the Konvikt —wrote: "I sat as first violin, and behind me, stand-

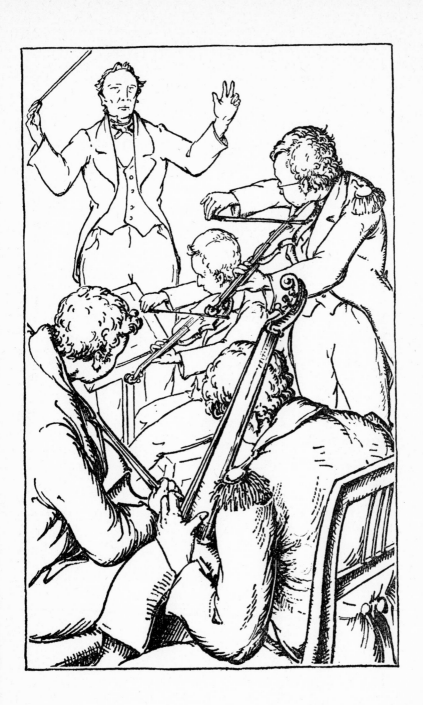

ing, little Schubert played from the same notes. Very
soon I became aware that the little musician played
in far better time than I did. This drew my attention
to him, and I noticed how the silent boy, who generally appeared to be indifferent and uninterested, was
carried away by the beauty of the music we performed. . . ."

At the close of the rehearsal, the music director
motioned to Franz to remain. When the others had
left he said: "It would be a great help if you would
take charge of the music for me—set up the stands
and see that each candle is snuffed and long enough
to last through the rehearsal."

Franz was quite willing, and he proved so quick
in sorting the music and putting it away that Herr
Ruziczka was delighted.

"I think you must like music!" he said to the
boy with a genial smile.

Franz blushed and stammered. "Oh, but I do,
Herr Musikdirektor—more than anything else."

Ruziczka smiled again. "Then I shall give you
special instruction—both on the piano and the violin.
And in counterpoint also."

Franz left the Music Room walking on air.

A few days later, as Josef Spaun went by the Music Room, he heard someone playing a Mozart sonata. This surprised him, for as a rule no one bothered with music at the Konvikt outside of school hours. He opened the door a crack and looked in. Franz turned from the piano in confusion.

"I wondered who was playing," Spaun said with a friendly smile. "It sounded very well."

For a moment Franz was quite overcome. He had not expected anyone to find him in the Music Room, least of all Josef Spaun, who was looked up to by every pupil in the Konvikt! The older boy seemed so apart from the rest, and so much more dignified, that Schubert had never dared hope he would notice an insignificant new pupil—let alone talk with him as an equal.

"Do you like Mozart?" Spaun continued, coming into the room and closing the door behind him.

Only one thing could make Franz forget his natural shyness and express himself in words, and that was music.

"There is no one like Mozart!" he answered fervently. "He is the greatest of all composers. You can hear the angels singing in his music—" He stopped short, as if afraid he had said too much, then continued in quieter tones: "But it is difficult to play Mozart well."

Spaun listened to Franz in surprise. He had

never known an eleven-year-old boy with such a feeling for music.

"Why do you come here alone, instead of playing games with the other boys?"

Franz blushed crimson and looked down at the floor. "I would rather make music," he answered in a low tone, almost as if he were admitting a fault.

"Why, so would I!" Spaun cried with enthusiasm. "I have always loved music better than anything else. You know," he continued with a touch of pride, "I organized the school orchestra here. At first Herr Direktor Lang insisted there wasn't money enough to buy music, and I used my allowance for the orchestra parts." He smiled ruefully. "Last year, for instance. . . ."

"Yes?" said Franz eagerly, all his self-consciousness forgotten.

"Well—" Spaun continued, "I had spent all my allowance for music. Then my father sent me money to buy a ticket back to our home in Linz for the summer holidays, and on my way to the coach, what should I see in the window of a music-shop but a new symphony by Herr van Beethoven? Of course I couldn't resist *that!*"

"Of course not," Franz echoed with beaming approval.

"And so," Spaun concluded, "having used the

ticket money to buy the score, there was nothing for it but to walk all the way back to Linz."

Franz laughed. "But it was worth it, now, wasn't it? Herr van Beethoven is a great composer —one of the greatest. You know," he continued in a burst of confidence, "*I* should like to write music. But who after Beethoven dare try?" Unconsciously his fingers fell on the piano and he began to play very softly.

"What are you playing there?" Spaun asked with sudden interest. "Why—it's beautiful! Did that come out of your head?"

Franz smiled in reply. "My head is always full of music," he answered simply.

"And do you write it down?" the older boy asked.

Young Schubert's face clouded over. "My father doesn't approve," he admitted with a gloomy frown. "He has forbidden me to write music. He says it is a waste of time."

Spaun was indignant. "It would be a far greater waste *not* to! That tune you played just now, for instance. . . ."

Franz nodded. "I have a few notes here." He reached into his pocket and pulled out a crumpled, clumsily ruled piece of paper. As he smoothed it out he sighed: "If only music-paper didn't cost so much! It takes so long to rule ordinary paper."

Spaun looked at the boy in amazement, almost in awe. To be able to compose music, and not have the means to buy paper on which to write it down! He, whose family had always provided him with a liberal allowance, could not understand such a situation.

Just then the bell for supper rang loudly through the house.

"Will you play for me again—soon?" Spaun asked.

His eyes alight with pleasure, Franz answered eagerly: "To be sure I will—*gladly!*"

A few days later Franz noticed a strange, subdued excitement in the school atmosphere. Groups of boys began whispering together in corners, and he couldn't imagine what it was all about until Holzapfel took him aside and explained.

"The Old Man has been on a rampage again!" he whispered, then added, as Franz looked blank: "The Herr Direktor—he birched Michael Senn. . . ."

"What for?" Young Schubert's eyes were full of dismay.

"Well, that's just it. It wasn't his fault. Really it was all because of Prefect Walch's snooping around and spreading false tales. But Senn wouldn't tell, so the Herr Direktor locked him up in the school prison. And Franz Eckel was so indignant that he let him out."

Franz nodded with a full appreciation of the gravity of the offense. Birching was common in those days; most of the boys felt the headmaster's rod sooner or later. And it was not unusual to be put into the school's prison, with nothing but bread and water. Insubordination, however, was considered a very serious matter.

"Herr Direktor Lang has announced that both Senn and Eckel will have to be expelled," Holzapfel continued, "and the rest of the boys say they will all leave if that happens. Unless Spaun can make the Herr Direktor listen to reason. . . ."

Just then the door of the principal's room opened, and Spaun came out. He was smiling, and the students who waited to hear the verdict gave a sigh of relief. Herr Lang had been persuaded to reconsider his decision, and the day was saved.

There were occasional rebellions against the harsh discipline at the Konvikt, but Franz never took part in these. Writing his recollections of Schubert in later years, Eckel said: "Professors and colleagues alike praised him for his sober conduct, which never led him into quarrels and never gave cause for them. Nor do I remember that Schubert ever received a disciplinary punishment. Everybody honored him, because he had already manifested unusual musical talent. . . ."

Franz was just dropping off to sleep that night when he heard a slight sound at the door. The moonlight was streaming in and he could just make out the figure of a tall youth tiptoeing through the dormitory in his nightclothes. He stopped at young Schubert's bed.

"Are you sleeping, Franz?" Josef Spaun whispered. "Listen—I have had a message from home, and must go back for a few days early tomorrow morning. Before I leave I want to give you this." He thrust a roll of paper into Franz's hand, and left as silently as he had come.

Franz opened the roll and examined it by the light of the moon.

Six large sheets of beautifully ruled music-paper!

Franz continued to spend most of his spare time in the Music Room, writing down and playing the melodies that were constantly urging him to expression. Some of the boys at the Konvikt kept a journal, or diary, of their ideas; but Franz wrote his thoughts down in music. For what came to others in terms of words was in his mind translated into lyrical songs, tender minuets, or somber *Trauer* marches.

One day as he was working hard at a new composition, Josef Spaun—whose absence from school had been only a short one—came in. He frequently dropped around to hear what Franz had written.

"How goes it, my friend?" he asked, stretching himself out on one of the wooden benches. *"Gibt's neues?*—have you anything new?"

Franz never minded when Spaun interrupted him. "I have a wonderful idea for a Fantasia," he said. "It will have twelve movements. The first is nearly completed."

"Good!" Josef applauded. "I must hear it. But just a moment," he called as Franz started with his manuscript for the piano. "You know you made me promise not to tell anyone about your composing? Well, it's got around somehow; at least Holzapfel and Eckel suspect why you shut yourself up here all the time. This morning they waylaid me in the hall, and—"

Before he could finish his sentence the door burst open, and in rushed the young gentlemen in question.

"Here he is!" they cried. "The cat is out of the bag, Franz. We know now why you will never play games with us!"

Franz blushed and tried to hide his manuscript. He looked as shamefaced as if he had been caught in

some disgraceful act.   But the boys were only teasing; actually they had a very deep appreciation of
music, and soon they persuaded young Schubert to
play some of his pieces for them.

When he had finished they were loud in their
praises, and so genuinely enthusiastic about his work
that Franz felt all warm and glowing.   He wondered
if he had been wrong in trying to keep his music to
himself.   It was very gratifying to have the approval
of friends!

The Music Room now became the gathering
place of a small group of real music-lovers.   Princi-
pally they came to hear Franz, but sometimes they
brought their own instruments and played and sang
together.   Then Franz would withdraw to a corner
and work quietly away at his music-writing.   Even
when the noise was loudest it did not seem to bother
him.

As a youth, Schubert lived for the most part in an inner
meditative life [wrote Eckel about this period], which seldom expressed itself to the world except in music.   Even
with his own most intimate friends, among whom at the
time were Anton Holzapfel and I, who read and sang his
first songs composed at the town Konvikt almost before the
paper was dry, he was scant of words.   He was almost entirely uncommunicative except about things which concerned
the Divine Muse to which he dedicated his short but complete life, and whose favorite he was.

An innate but tactful measure of seriousness and calm,

friendliness and good nature, admitted neither of friendship nor enmity such as exists usually among boys and youths at educational institutions—the less so since Schubert, except in study and class time, spent almost all hours granted for recreation in the Music Room, mostly alone. . . .

Also, during the pupils' walks he kept himself mostly apart, his head bent downwards, looking in front of him, his hands folded across his back, his fingers moving as if playing on the keys. Withdrawn into himself he walked as if in deep meditation. I never saw him in a passion. He was always vivacious, although this was manifested more in facial expression than in words, which were usually few in number and revealed a deep fund of humor. I saw him laugh but seldom, but he often smiled, sometimes without reason, as if it were the reflex of the thoughts passing in his mind. . . .

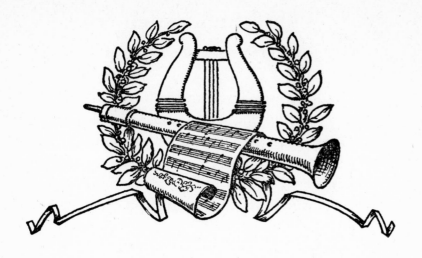

CHAPTER V

Napoleon the Conqueror

IN 1805 Vienna had been visited by one of the worst calamities of its history. Napoleon Bonaparte, apparently set on conquering all of Europe, had attacked Austria; he met with little resistance, and soon his victorious army marched into Vienna.

Terrible tales had been spread about the savagery of the French troops. When they poured into the city the people were too frightened to venture into the streets, but they watched from behind their shuttered windows as Napoleon's army—many of them badly wounded, others with their ears cut off by the Russians—swarmed in like a plague of locusts. The soldiers demanded food from every household, and went through the town looting and burning down houses wherever they passed.

Nothing was left for the people themselves; many starved to death, and—as if this were not enough—Bonaparte imposed heavy taxes and took away what little money was left in the city. One wealthy Austrian tried to save his fortune by investing it in wine. The soldiers came and drank the wine all up!

The people of Vienna never forgot these indignities; they were determined to revenge themselves, and four years later, when Napoleon's campaign in Spain seemed to be turning badly, the Austrians decided that this would be a good time to strike a blow against their weakened French foe.

But Napoleon Bonaparte was invincible. Once more he overcame all resistance, and early in May reached the environs of Vienna and demanded the surrender of the city.

Franz Schubert had been at the Konvikt just six months when Napoleon and his troops arrived at the gates of Vienna. The people were in a state of terrified excitement; it was rumored that the Austrian army had surrendered, yet many of the Viennese thought it might still be possible to save their city. In any case they felt they would rather die fighting than undergo the terrors of another occupation.

Groups of citizens began to arm themselves;

they built barricades in the city streets, hoping to stop the advance of the French invaders. A call was sent out for volunteers, and the students of the University, across from the Konvikt, formed a company of their own. When news of this reached the Konvikt, the older boys there were determined to go out and join in the defense.

"Can we sit here like helpless women and children," cried Senn, addressing a group of students who had gathered in the Music Room, "and let our city be looted again by a lot of barbarians?"

"*No!*" came the answer from a dozen throats.

"But will the Herr Direktor let us go?" a timid voice demanded.

"We'll not ask him! Vienna's safety is the only thing that matters. Come—all those who would be brave soldiers. The least we can do is to enlist."

Director Lang was furious when he found that the boys had gone. He felt a serious responsibility towards his students' parents for keeping their sons in safety, and also he knew only too well the futility of resisting the powerful French forces. When the young patriots returned from enlisting—proud as peacocks over their cockades of red and white ribbon which marked them full-fledged recruits, Herr Lang met them at the door and sent them to their rooms where they were all locked in.

By this time, however, the boys were too fired

with zeal for their city's salvation to respect any minor authority. They climbed through the windows and went off to drill. Prefect Walch reported the matter to Director Lang.

There was only one hope of saving the young rebels, the Konvikt's principal decided. If Archduke Rudolph, in charge of the city's defense, could be made to intervene. . . . Hastily he wrote a letter, explaining the situation.

Then he remembered that Otto, his servant, had also enlisted. Dare he entrust one of the boys with such an important mission? Yes—there was one who had proved himself especially reliable.

A few minutes later, Franz, feeling very excited and important, and clutching tightly a large, official-looking letter, was on his way to the palace. If he had known that this letter spelled disgrace for his comrades, he might not have been so eager to fulfill his commission.

There was no fighting as yet, but the streets were filled with anxious people, and he could not get through some of the blockaded highways. He was stopped several times, but when he showed his letter to the Archduke they let him pass.

Archduke Rudolph was pacing up and down his study when Franz was finally admitted to his presence.

"It is folly to resist the French any further," he

was saying to the Prime Minister. "If we continue
to fight, Napoleon will simply lay the city waste and
massacre all the people. No—our Emperor is right;
if the people lay down their arms at once perhaps
Bonaparte will be more lenient in his peace demands."

"It will not be so easy to stop the citizens now
that their passion is aroused," the Prime Minister
murmured.

When the Archduke read Herr Lang's letter, a
smile hovered at the corner of his mouth. "Young
hot-heads!" he said, half affectionately. "But Lang
is right—they still need discipline." He questioned
Franz about the details of the rebellion, then
scratched an order on a piece of paper, sealed it
quickly, and called a waiting sentry. "Take this to
the captain of the volunteers," he commanded.

Franz's heart was very heavy as he walked back
to the Konvikt. But he was less concerned over the
prospect of Vienna's downfall than over the fate
which awaited his comrades.

The young rebels had already been brought back
to the Konvikt by the time he reached the school.
Herr Lang was not so severe as he might have been,
but he locked the boys in their rooms for several days.

Napoleon's spies had reported to him that preparations were being made in Vienna to resist his occupation.

The "Little Corporal", who now called himself "Emperor of the French", was indignant. "Crazy fools—do they think they can defy my army? Do they believe their unorganized rabble has a chance to hold back seasoned veterans?"

It was early in May, and in contrast to the bloody scenes of warfare, the countryside around Vienna had never been so beautiful. Napoleon had ordered a luxurious tent set up for his use outside the city gates; his army was encamped around him, waiting for the order to march in and occupy the city.

"Perhaps if these hot-blooded Viennese get a taste of our cannon they will not be so eager to resist," Napoleon continued. "At nightfall we will begin the attack."

That evening the young members of the orchestra at the Konvikt were just finishing the Overture to Mozart's *Magic Flute* when they heard a great explosion in the distance. With one accord everyone rushed out into the square before the school. By now Napoleon's cannon balls were falling fast and thick, and their flight through the skies caused the boys as much excitement as if this had been a display of fireworks arranged especially for their amusement.

Suddenly a bomb fell right into the large fountain of the University Square. By a happy miracle no one was hurt.

"Get down into the cellar, all of you!" Director Lang shouted, ordering all the boys into the house. "Prefect Walch, go up and release the young men who are locked in their rooms, and see that they also come down into the cellar."

The students were indignant over the bombardment. "The Frenchies are afraid to come into the city and fight like men," they said scornfully. "We'd soon show them if they did! Cowards. . . ."

Franz told the boys what he had heard at the palace. "The Archduke says that it would be folly to resist. If the people had only listened to him, Napoleon would not have turned his cannon on the city."

"Does he think we're going to sit quietly by and let those French bandits pillage our Vienna a second time—and loot our homes? A fine lot of cowards we should be!"

"But—" Franz began.

Just as he opened his mouth to speak, a terrific crash rocked the walls of the Konvikt School; they could hear bricks falling and ceilings collapsing over their heads. A cloud of dust filtered down into the cellar where the boys were huddled in a dark corner. No one dared to move for several minutes after the explosion.

Then Director Lang stepped forward. "I will go up and investigate," he said.

Spaun stood up. "Let me go with you, Herr Direktor. There may be danger."

"And I will come too—" "And I—" "And I—" chorused the group that had been so eager to fight. Prefect Walch, however, did not show his face; he was still cowering beneath the stairs.

But Herr Lang would not allow anyone to accompany him. He was gone for some time, and during his absence the bombardment ceased. When the Director returned everyone crowded around him to learn what had happened.

"A bomb fell through the roof," he told them. "It passed through several stories and finally exploded in Prefect Walch's room."

There was silence, as each one realized what they had all escaped. Then Holzapfel whispered in Franz's ear: "All the same, it's too bad old Walch wasn't in his room!"

The following day it was learned that the Austrian Emperor had sent a peace messenger to Napoleon, saying that the city would offer no further resistance, and would be ready to receive the conqueror with open gates and a fitting ceremony of submission.

Sadly the Viennese put away their guns and clubs and pulled down the barricades in the streets. In place of these defenses the people were commanded to string up banners of welcome, and decorate their houses with flowers and green boughs.

Napoleon announced that he would make a triumphal entry into Vienna on May 14th. Early that morning the people began to crowd into the streets; everyone was anxious for a glimpse of the notorious Napoleon Bonaparte and his redoubtable troops. The French Emperor had promised that this time there would be no looting or violence of any kind.

The boys of the Konvikt, with the exception of the young patriots who were still in disgrace, were given a half holiday to witness the festivities.

"You can count it a lesson in history," Herr Lang told them, with a certain bitter humor.

The main ceremony was to take place in the big central square before the Cathedral of St. Stephen. Here a canopied platform hung with velvet curtains and carpeted in crimson had been erected. In token of submission the Austrian Emperor himself was to acclaim the conqueror; he was to present the French ruler with the keys of the city, and seat him in his place on the improvised throne. The large iron key which opened the main gate of Vienna had been specially gilded for the occasion.

Franz and his friend Holzapfel were up before daybreak on the eventful morning. They had a secret scheme which they were anxious to try out. Stuffing some bread and cheese in their pockets, they made their way to the Stefanplatz and climbed to the roof of one of the neighboring buildings. From this vantage point they could look directly down on the activities below and see everything that took place.

Napoleon had sent word that he wished to review the Imperial Viennese Guard, and shortly after the boys had climbed to their roof top, the Emperor's special troops, magnificent in their best dress uniforms, began to assemble in the square. Soon the place was packed with spectators. For the most part it was a good-natured crowd. The Viennese were too light-hearted to be long downcast, and in spite of the seriousness of the moment they took this event in holiday spirit, much as they would any spectacle designed for their special entertainment.

Franz and "Wooden-Apple" crouched in the shadow of a tall chimney-pot. All at once the latter clutched his companion. "Look, Franz! Do you see that short, heavy-set man with the bushy black hair and the old, dilapidated hat?"

Franz turned his gaze in the direction Holzapfel indicated. "Do you mean the one with his arms crossed who is frowning so fiercely?"

"Yes. I think—I am almost sure it is Herr van Beethoven."

Franz peered through his steel-rimmed spectacles with emotion. To him, Beethoven was even greater than Napoleon.

"They say that Beethoven hates Napoleon," Holzapfel declared. "My father knows Carl Czerny, who studied with Beethoven, and he said that his master had once admired Bonaparte tremendously. But when he proclaimed himself Emperor of the French, Beethoven insisted that this marked him as a tyrant."

Franz looked down at the frowning figure with awe. To be able to compose as Beethoven did— surely nothing in the world could be so wonderful as that. By comparison, what was the conquering of a few countries—of the whole world, for that matter? For war, Franz thought to himself, means bitter tragedy and suffering, but music brings joy and inspiration to the hearts of mankind.

"You know," Holzapfel went on, "Beethoven's Third Symphony—the one they call the *Eroica?*"

"Yes," Franz replied, still lost in his thoughts.

"Herr Czerny said that Beethoven originally composed that symphony in honor of Napoleon, but that when Bonaparte declared himself Emperor of the French, Beethoven tore off the dedication of the score—indeed, he came near to destroying the whole work!"

A harsh blare of trumpets sounded in the square below. "They are coming!" Holzapfel cried in high excitement. He leaned so far forward that he almost lost his balance and would have slid down into the square below if Franz had not grabbed him by one arm and pulled him back.

From the distance came an answering fanfare from the French horns. The Austrian Emperor, surrounded by the members of his personal staff, took his place on the improvised throne. Then came an endless procession of Napoleon's troops, infantry and cavalry, and great cannons drawn by many horses. They filed past the platform and then went on down a side street.

This continued for so long that the two boys, crouched in their uncomfortable vantage point, wondered if they could manage to stick it out until the central figure—the great Napoleon himself—should arrive.

At last there was a murmur through the crowd, and people strained their necks to look over the shoulders of those in front of them. Then they pressed back in an effort to escape flying hoofs. Napoleon's special guard charged into the square on prancing black horses. Close behind them a small, solitary figure, seated on a magnificent white horse, and wearing a flowing white broadcloth cape thrown over one shoulder, advanced slowly to the center of the Stefanplatz.

Bonaparte looked haughtily about him. He answered the Austrian Emperor's deep bow with a casual wave of his hand, and then passed slowly up and down the ranks of the Imperial Guard, examining them with such a hostile, contemptuous air that the excited whispering of the people died down into an ominous silence.

What followed was so sudden and so unexpected that the two boys from the Konvikt could hardly tell later how it happened.

A young man, little more than a boy, suddenly broke through the crowds lining the square and threw himself at Napoleon, knife in hand. But before he could plunge this into the conqueror's heart two of the French generals seized the youth and threw him to the ground.

Napoleon seemed quite unmoved. "Why did you want to kill me?" he asked the reckless youth. "What harm have I done you?"

The boy looked up at him with somber eyes. "You are the oppressor of my country," he said fiercely. "You are the tyrant of the whole world. To have put you to death would have been the highest glory of a man of honor."

Bonaparte only laughed and turned away. The youth was led off under a heavy guard, and passed close beneath the house where Franz and Holzapfel watched from the roof.   Just around the corner the guards stood the boy up against the wall.   There was a volley of shots. . . . The figure of the boy crumpled to the ground.

Franz felt suddenly ill.   "Let's get back to the Konvikt," he whispered to his companion.

Napoleon installed himself in the castle of Schönbrunn.   He taxed the people heavily, and deprived them of so many privileges that Vienna, which had been the gayest city in Europe, now became like a mournful shadow of its former carefree self.

For five long months the French conqueror remained at Schönbrunn.   Then finally in October the long-drawn-out peace negotiations were concluded, and Bonaparte returned to Paris.

The people drew a long sigh of relief.   Once more there was laughter and merrymaking in Vienna.

CHAPTER VI

Franz in Disgrace

THE boys of the Konvikt orchestra were all
assembled on the evening of their return
from the summer holidays in 1810, ready
to begin their usual hour of music. But
the first violin stand was empty.

"You all know," Herr Ruziczka informed them,
"that Herr Spaun is no longer with us. He has finished his studies in Vienna and returned to Linz. In
his place—" He paused and looked around the
orchestra. The boys began to whisper among themselves, but there was not much doubt in their minds
who would succeed Spaun.

79

"In his place," Herr Ruziczka continued, "I appoint Franz Schubert. He will be concertmaster and conduct the orchestra whenever I am absent."

Franz was delighted at his promotion, though it hardly made up to him for the loss of his best friend. He and Spaun had been so close to each other during their years at the Konvikt that Franz did not see how he could get along without this sympathetic companionship.

To console himself, Franz plunged into a new composition. It was the most ambitious work he had ever undertaken: a long, elaborate church cantata called *Hagars Klage* (Hagar's Lament) and he became so absorbed in his task that not only every minute of his free time was given to it, but hours that should have been spent in schoolwork were devoted to the cantata.

When it was finally completed Franz took the long manuscript to Herr Ruziczka.

The music director was filled with wonder. Young Schubert's extraordinary talent had always amazed him. He had long suspected that there was nothing further he could teach his pupil. Now, after seeing the score of *Hagars Klage*, he was sure of it.

"It is time, my boy," he said, polishing his spectacles vigorously, "that I took you to Signor Salieri. He is the only teacher in Vienna from whom you may still learn something."

Antonio Salieri was an Italian by birth, but most of his life had been spent in Vienna, and he was very popular there. He was the composer of a number of operas, which he himself conducted at the Royal Opera House, and the Emperor had appointed him to the highest musical post in Austria. He was *Hofkapellmeister* or "Court Director of Music", and lived in an elegant apartment in a wing of the Emperor's palace.

When Ruziczka, accompanied by Franz, knocked at the great Salieri's door, it was opened by an imposing footman in bright-colored livery.

"Tell your master that Herr Ruziczka, Court organist and director of music at the Konvikt School, would like to speak with him," said the music director in the most imposing manner he could assume.

The footman bowed and disappeared into an inner room. In a moment he returned. "His Honor the Kapellmeister is at present engaged with his hairdresser. But if you care to step in he will see you."

Ruziczka motioned to Franz to wait for him in the anteroom while he followed the footman. The door was left ajar, and Franz could hear the two men's conversation.

"Ah, my fr-r-riend!" he heard a foreign voice exclaim. (Salieri never learned to speak German properly. Even at the end of his life, if anyone remarked about that fact he would say: "But I have only been in Austria such a short time—not more than fifty years!")

"It is much time that you did not come to see me," Salieri went on. ("*You*—Benvenuto—a little more careful with those curling irons!")

"My sorrow, Your Honor," Ruziczka murmured. "In addition to the church services I am very busy teaching at the Konvikt."

"Yes, yes—I know. How goes it now? Have you clever pupils?"

"That is just what I came to talk to you about, Herr Kapellmeister. There is one boy at the Konvikt who is most exceptional. You may remember—I have spoken to you about him before. He is the one who passed the examinations so brilliantly in 1808— Franz Schubert by name. Do you recall?"

There was a moment's silence. Then—"Ai-i-i, Benvenuto, attention! Yes, I believe I do remember. Has the boy turned out as well as you expected?"

"Better, Your Honor, much better. In fact—" He lowered his voice and Franz could hear only an occasional word. "I can teach him nothing . . . composes . . . seems to have learned everything from God. . . ."

"So-o-o? That is extraordinary. I must hear this young prodigy."

"As a matter of fact, I have brought the boy with me." Herr Ruziczka's voice grew louder and

Franz realized he was coming to the door. "He is waiting now in the anteroom. If you will permit me—"

Franz clutched his three-cornered hat in both hands and stood up with a beating heart. Through the open door he could see the small, dapper figure of the celebrated Italian. A servant was holding out for him an elegant coat of plum-colored brocade with lace ruffles at the cuffs, while Benvenuto, the hairdresser, stood off to admire the curls he had just finished arranging on his master's elaborate gray wig. Salieri, smiling at his own reflection in the mirror, sauntered into the anteroom. He looked critically at the boy who was bowing before him.

"He doesn't *look* very intelligent!" he muttered over his shoulder to Ruziczka.

Certainly young Franz Schubert was not very attractive in appearance. Short and stocky, his Konvikt School uniform too tight for him and too long in the sleeves and trousers, his hair a shock of unruly curls, and his nearsighted eyes blinking behind their steel-rimmed spectacles—no one would have suspected that here was a boy destined to become one of the world's greatest composers.

"So-o-o, you wish to become musician?" Salieri asked, not unkindly.

Franz blushed furiously. "Yes, your Honor," he stammered.

Salieri led the way into his drawing-room. Franz, who had never known any but the most humble surroundings, drew his breath in wonder as he looked around the large room: long french windows curtained with heavy red damask opened out on the palace gardens; gilt chairs stood around the hall reflected in the highly polished parquet floor; an ornate crystal chandelier hung from the high ceiling and sparkled in the sunlight like a great cluster of diamonds. But to Franz most marvelous of all was the large pianoforte of gilt painted with pastoral scenes, and so magnificent that he wondered how anyone would dare touch such an instrument, let alone perform on it.

Salieri seated himself at the piano and played a simple theme. "See what you can make of this," he said, motioning to Franz to take his place.

Young Schubert sat for a moment with his eyes closed. Then he began to improvise on the theme, weaving the brief tune into all sorts of variations. The clear, fine tone of the piano, so different from any he had ever played on before, inspired him to unusual heights; he forgot the unaccustomed splendor of his surroundings, and lost himself in the music.

Salieri and Ruziczka were whispering together in a corner. "Remarkable—really remarkable!" said the Italian. When Schubert stopped playing, the

little Kapellmeister shouted, "Bravo!   You have true
—how do you say?—true musical understanding."

Franz saw that Ruziczka had given him the
score to *Hagar's Lament*.   "You wish to—ah—*compose?*"   Salieri began to turn over the pages, and as
he went through the manuscript his expression became more and more amazed.

"*Incredibile!*" he muttered in his own tongue.
"*Non ho mai veduto.* . . . Of course—" He
slashed with his pencil through certain passages.
"—there are errors, but *in tutto* it is excellent.   R-re-
markable!   Your pupil," he said, looking up at the
Court organist, "is a cr-redit to you, my friend!"

Ruziczka cleared his throat.   "I was sure Your
Honor would recognize that fact," he said eagerly,
watching the Italian to see his reaction.   "Franz
Schubert would be a credit to any teacher."

Salieri tapped his finger thoughtfully against his
lips.   "You are right . . ."   He turned to Franz.
"Perhaps you would like to study with me, yes?"

Young Schubert was too bashful to speak, but before he and Herr Ruziczka concluded their visit it
was arranged that Franz should come to Salieri twice
a week for lessons.

A few months later Franz was returning from a lesson with Salieri when, just as he entered the door, Prefect Walch came sidling up to him.

"The Herr Direktor requests your presence, Herr Schubert," he said with a look full of sly significance.

Franz hurried at once to Director Lang's private parlor. The curtains were drawn and the big porcelain stove in the corner made the room almost suffocatingly hot.

"Sit down, my boy," the principal said curtly. "I want to talk to you." He pulled out a sheaf of papers from a drawer in the table beside him, and began looking them over. "It seems that your grades are not satisfactory. Not at all satisfactory," he repeated, looking at Franz over the top of his spectacles.

Franz shifted the large manuscript of *Hagar's Lament* under his arm with a very guilty feeling. "Yes, sir," he said in a small voice.

"I am disappointed in you," Herr Lang continued. "You can do better than this, I know."

"Yes, sir," Franz repeated meekly. "I will try, Herr Direktor."

"I should be sorry to see you leave the Konvikt," the principal added in a significant tone; "your music is a credit to this institution. But you must not forget that other studies have just as much importance, if not more."

Franz left Herr Lang's room with a firm determination to work harder at his regular studies. But the score of *Hagar's Lament* proved too much of a temptation. That evening, instead of devoting himself to the next day's lessons, he slipped into the Music Room. No one saw him go in but Prefect Walch. . . .

In a few moments the boy was deep in his manuscript. Yes, Salieri had been right to cut out this passage. But *this* one—*no!* It was harmonically correct. Why? . . .

"What are you doing, Franz?" Herr Direktor Lang asked, coming into the room. Franz jumped in guilty surprise. Herr Lang was never known to leave his own apartment in the evening, since Prefect Walch was on duty at that time.

The principal came over and examined the bulky score in young Schubert's hands. "Is this your work?" The boy had to admit it was. "Then I understand why your studies have suffered." Herr Lang went on leafing through the long composition. Then he looked severely at Franz. "Your father warned me that you took music too seriously for your own good. He must be told of this."

A few days later Herr Schubert came to the school in high indignation.

"So this is the way you obey my orders!" he said to the unfortunate Franz. "Just because I was persuaded to let you study with Signor Salieri—more because of his reputation than anything else—you repay me by neglecting your studies."

"I will do better . . ." Franz replied meekly.

"I should hope so!" sputtered the irate parent. "If it's not too late already. Don't you know that if you fail to maintain a high standard in your regular studies you will be dismissed from the Konvikt? You seem to think that music is the only thing that matters. Have you forgotten what the Emperor said? 'Singing and music are of secondary importance. Good manners and diligence in studies, however, are of primary importance, and an essential duty in those who wish to enjoy the tenure of a scholarship.' "

Father Schubert looked severely at Franz. " 'Music is of *secondary* importance,' his Highness says, and he also states very clearly that you will lose your scholarship if you are not diligent in your studies."

Franz hung his head, while his father continued in bitter tones: "Do you realize what that would mean —to lose your scholarship? Your whole career would be spoiled. How can you expect to get a teacher's certificate without a proper education?"

The boy suddenly found his voice. "But I don't *want* to be a schoolteacher, Father," he said with sudden daring.

"What!" Herr Schubert cried in outraged astonishment. "Why, I thought it had always been understood. Pray, then, what *do* you want to be?"

Franz hesitated. "I want to compose music," he answered slowly.

Father Schubert looked at the boy as if he had lost his mind. "Foolishness!" he exploded. "Writing music is no kind of career. I thought you had gotten that silly idea out of your head. Until you do"—his voice was grim—"I don't want to see you again. You needn't come home until you promise me you will give up this time-wasting infatuation."

A stubborn light crept into Franz's usually gentle eyes. "Very well, Father," he answered. "I will stay away if you wish. But," he added defiantly, "I cannot give up music. . . ."

Herr Schubert was true to his word: he forbade the house to his youngest son and did not even allow him to see his mother. Franz was very unhappy. He missed the weekly trips home more than he was willing to admit; but most of all he longed to see his mother.   She had not been very strong lately.

Young Schubert missed the good dinners, too. The food at the Konvikt was poor in quality and in the way it was cooked, and there was hardly enough to satisfy the appetites of growing boys.   Franz's round figure bore witness to his fondness for good things to eat!

After several weeks in which he really suffered from his privations, he wrote to his brother Ferdinand:

24th November, 1812

Let me bring out at once what is on my mind, so that I may come to the point and not just meander coyly around it.   For a long time now I have thought over my position and have found it on the whole passably good, though there is still room for improvement here and there.   You know from experience how sometimes one wants to eat a roll and a few apples, and all the more when after a modest dinner one can only look forward to a wretched supper 8½ hours later.   This persistent wish troubles me more and more, and I must, *nolens volens*, hit upon a way of getting rid of it. The few groschen that my father allows me are all spent— the devil knows how—in the first few days.   What am I to do for the rest of the time?   "They who put their trust in Thee shall not be confounded."   So I thought: How would it be if you were to let me have a few kreutzers each month? You would not really feel it, while I should consider myself lucky and be quite satisfied in my cloistral retreat.   As I said before, I rely on the words of the Apostle Matthew where he says: "He that hath two coats let him give one to the poor." Meantime I hope that you will lend an ear to the incessantly calling voice of your

Loving, hopeful, once again poor,
and not to be forgotten brother,

Franz.

Months passed, and Father Schubert proved unrelenting. Franz, on his side, was equally stubborn; he devoted more time to his studies, and was able to keep his scholarship at the Konvikt, but he could not resist writing music.

And because he was fulfilling this compelling desire of his heart, he managed in spite of his separation from his family to be reasonably happy. Even the privations and discomforts of his life at the Konvikt did not disturb him, for whenever he had a spare hour he could escape into a beautiful world of his own constructing.

Every day there would be some new inspiration, and as soon as he had written it down he would play it for his friends. Schubert was never happy until he had shared his music with his friends. Their affection and approval were a necessity to his gentle, confiding nature. He never minded when they interrupted his work. Holzapfel, Senn, and Stadler would burst into the Music Room with an eager: "What have you written today, Franz? Quick, to the piano and let us hear it!"

Albert Stadler has left a description of Schubert's method of composing:

It was interesting to see him compose. Very rarely did he use the pianoforte. He often said that this would interrupt the train of his thoughts. Quietly and little troubled by the talking and noise of his fellow students, unavoidable at the Konvikt, he sat at his little table, a sheet of notepaper in front of him, and closely stooped over that and the textbook (he was very shortsighted), chewing the pen, sometimes playing (as if trying a passage) with his fingers on the table, and writing easily and fluently without many corrections, as if it had to be just so and not otherwise. . . .

Schubert wrote nine ambitious compositions that year, including an overture, two string quartets, a sonata, and a long dramatic song called *Der Vatermörder*. This last tells of a son who is consumed with a desire to murder his father, but finally becomes conscience-stricken at such evil thoughts. Evidently Franz, in spite of his mild and forgiving nature, felt an unconscious resentment against his own father which expressed itself through the only medium he knew.

In 1811 Josef Spaun, now a young man of twenty-three, was appointed to a government position and came back to Vienna to live. Franz was overjoyed at his friend's return. When Spaun came to visit the Konvikt, he greeted Schubert with—"Can you guess what I have brought you?" and handed him a package.

"*Music-paper!*" Franz cried in delight. "To think that you should remember after all this time. I never have enough," he continued ruefully. "The ideas come so fast, and it takes so much paper to set them down on."

Spaun came frequently to visit Franz and as in the past kept him supplied with music-paper. And Franz, although he now devoted more time to his regular studies, continued to write quantities of music.

On Corpus Christi day in late May of 1812, the choirboys were just preparing to leave for early Mass at the Imperial Chapel when Karl Schubert came running up the steps of the Konvikt. Franz had not seen his brother for months, and he was delighted at this unexpected visit, until suddenly he noticed the tragic expression on Karl's face.

"What *is* it, Karl?" he cried, hardly daring to ask.

Karl had hurried so fast that he could hardly speak. "Our mother is very ill—they fear she cannot live. Father says you are to come at once."

As they hastened back to Lichtenthal, Karl told

his brother what had happened. There was an epidemic of typhus at that time. (This much-feared disease, always a menace because of the poor sanitation in Vienna, swept through the city at frequent intervals. Seventeen years later it was to cause the death of Franz Schubert himself.) Frau Schubert had not been well for some months, and she fell a ready victim to the deadly typhus. Herr Schubert, stubborn to the last, was not willing to notify Franz until he saw there was no hope. Elisabet, the "quiet, unpretentious woman . . . greatly loved by her children and esteemed by all", lay dying.

In later years Franz could never think of the hours that followed his homecoming without a sad, tight feeling in his heart. He had loved his mother very dearly. Whenever he spoke of her he always called her "the *good* mother".

Herr Schubert grieved deeply over his wife's death, and blamed himself for having kept Franz away from his mother for so long. What was more, echoes of the high esteem in which his son's music was held at the Konvikt must have reached Lichtenthal, for now the schoolmaster was willing to admit that there might be some good in Franz's composing.

Once again the boy began to spend his Sundays at home, and, as before, the afternoons were given to chamber music. Franz was now the recognized leader of the family quartet. His older brothers were quite willing to have him make suggestions and correct their playing, and even Father Schubert did not object when his youngest son would tactfully remark, "I think you've missed something here, sir!"

One day, with some misgivings, Franz brought a quartet of his own composing. Herr Schubert made no objection to playing it; he even praised the work, and Franz was so pleased that he forgot much of the resentment he had felt towards his father.

On Schoolmaster Schubert's birthday Franz brought him a beautifully written manuscript, tied in a roll with an elegant blue ribbon. It was a cantata inscribed:

For My Father's Name-Day

CHAPTER VII

Another Schoolmaster?

FRANZ was now fifteen years old, and he knew
that, since his voice would soon be changing,
he could not remain much longer in the Imperial Choir. He began to realize how much
it had meant to him all these years to sing in the
stately old Court Chapel. From his seat in the carved
choir-stall he could look up past high pillars to the
vaulted roof above, and toward the High Altar where
candles shone like stars in the shadows. The solemn
chanting, the incense-laden air, and the majestic
music of the organ all left a deep impression of mys-
tical beauty on the boy's sensitive nature.

One Sunday, a few months after his mother's death, Franz sang in the choir for the last time. Suddenly, in the midst of a solemn *Te Deum,* instead of the usual notes a strange noise came from his throat. He sounded absurdly like a crow! A suppressed titter ran through the choir, and young Schubert was so embarrassed that he wanted to crawl under his seat.

"Well, my boy," Herr Ruziczka said regretfully, as Franz, following the service was changing his vestments amidst the good-natured jeering of his fellow choristers, "I'm afraid your singing days are over. But I hope Director Lang will let you stay on at the Konvikt. We need you in the orchestra."

Franz himself doubted whether he would be allowed to remain. He knew that his class work had not been brilliant; even with the best of intentions music always seemed to come first with him. When, later on that same day, Herr Lang called him into his study, Franz waited anxiously to hear the verdict.

" 'If a boy distinguishes himself in morals and studies,' " Herr Lang quoted, " 'he is entitled to remain in the school even after his voice changes.' Now as to morals, Herr Schubert, I can testify that you have a good character."

"Thank you, sir," Franz murmured.

"But as to studies, I cannot say as much. Your record is only fair. Your arithmetic is especially weak."

Young Schubert looked very unhappy. He knew only too well his weakness in figures.

"However," the Director continued, "you have been such a credit to us in a musical way—particularly in the orchestra—that we have decided to let you stay on for the time being."

"Oh, *thank* you, Herr Direktor!" Franz cried joyfully.

(There is still in existence a copy of the Mass that was sung that morning in the Imperial Chapel of Vienna. On the flyleaf is written in an unknown boyish hand: "Franz Schubert crowed for the last time, July 26, 1812.")

During the months following Elisabet's death, Herr Schubert was in a state of bewildered despair. He had not realized how much the welfare of the household depended on his wife's quiet but efficient care, nor how he himself had looked to the sympathetic companionship and wise advice she was always ready to give him.

Little Theresa was only eleven years old when her mother died, too young to take charge of the house. The servant that Herr Schubert engaged was inefficient and slovenly; after his wife's fine cooking he could hardly eat the food that now came on the table. Everything at the *Schwarzen Rössl* was in disorder and confusion, and Herr Schubert felt lonely and unhappy. He finally decided that there was only one remedy for the situation. He must look for another wife.

Schoolmaster Schubert was fortunate in finding a young woman who filled his needs perfectly. Anna Kleyenbock was the daughter of a silk manufacturer, and although twenty years younger than her new husband (Elisabet had been seven years older) she proved a devoted and loving wife.

Anna was blessed with a gay, happy disposition, and she soon won the hearts of her five stepchildren. They were all present at the wedding; even Franz was allowed to come home from the Konvikt to celebrate the event. Father Schubert entered the date, April 13, 1813, in the big family Bible, opposite the tragic birth-and-death list of Elisabet's fourteen children. Later the names of five more sons and daughters were recorded in the Bible. Life was easier now in the Schubert household; Frau Anna brought a good dowry, and only one child of this second marriage died in infancy.

One Sunday in the late summer following Herr Schubert's second marriage Franz went home as usual to visit his family. When the dinner was over, and Frau Anna and little Theresa were putting away the dishes, Father Schubert cleared his throat loudly in a way he had when there was something important to discuss.

"It is high time, Franz," he said, "that we make plans for your future. The extension which Director Lang has given you will soon be up and you will have to leave the Konvikt."

Franz had been dreading this moment for some weeks. "I thought," he began, stuttering a little in his nervousness, "I hoped, at least, that Signor Salieri might recommend me for a position."

There was dead silence at the table. Ferdinand looked at Ignatz, and Karl stared anxiously at his father's face. Even Frau Anna, laughing with Theresa at one end of the table, was suddenly quiet. At last Herr Schubert spoke.

"Do I understand you to say," he remarked in icy tones, "that you wish to take a *musical* position?"

"Why, yes. I—that is," Franz stammered, "I had hoped it might be possible."

"Still that old obsession!" his father interrupted severely. Then, noting the obstinate gleam that appeared in his son's eyes, he changed the subject abruptly. "Have you reflected that on your next birthday you will be liable for military conscription?"

Franz knew this only too well. Conscription hung over the heads of all young men in Austria like a dark cloud or some terrible nightmare. Those who could buy their release, or bring influence to bear, might escape the dreaded service, but failing this they could be required to remain for as long as fourteen years in the Army. Franz had hoped that his short stature and poor eyesight would prevent him from being taken, but when he mentioned this, Father Schubert laughed.

"Only if you were a complete cripple would they excuse you," he said grimly. "Austria has been through so many wars that anything is now taken for cannon fodder. There is only one way for you to escape: the country still needs schoolteachers to train her young, almost as much as soldiers to fight for her glory, and teachers are excused from the Army."

Franz stared with somber eyes at Frau Anna's snowy tablecloth. He knew that it had always been his father's intention that all of his sons should follow his own profession. Herr Schubert needed them badly to assist him in his growing school. Ignatz had been a willing apprentice; Ferdinand made little objection; but Karl hated the idea almost as much as Franz did—he wanted to be an artist.

And Franz wanted to be a musician. At the same time he realized that a musical career would not

exempt him from military conscription. Just to think
of the horrors of war and the discomforts of a soldier's
life made him shudder. Anything would be better
than that. . . .

A last ray of hope occurred to Franz. "But
what of my inheritance from my mother? Won't
that be enough to buy my release from military
service?"

"My poor child, you do not understand the value
of money," Father Schubert said in a gentler tone.
"Your inheritance is chiefly tied up in this building
which your mother helped me to buy. As long as I
am here you can be assured of a position as assistant
teacher. The State will pay you forty gulden a quarter, and"—he coughed slightly and glanced towards
his wife—"I shall not charge you much for your
board. At least you will be safe from the hardships
of the Army."

Franz gave up. "Perhaps you are right,
Father," he said in a dull voice.

When Herr Schubert saw that he had won the
day all his ill humor vanished, and he became quite
genial and good-natured. "I have already spoken to
Herr Direktor Lang," he said, "and he has promised
to recommend you for the St. Anna's teachers' college."

In token of appreciation for his five years at the Konvikt, young Schubert decided to dedicate his first symphony to Director Lang. The latter's birthday came just as Franz was leaving for St. Anna's, so the symphony was rehearsed in secret, as a surprise for the event.

There was always a special celebration in honor of the Herr Direktor's *Geburtstag*. First the boys were given a fine and much-appreciated supper, and this was usually followed by some kind of entertainment.

On the evening of October 28th, the Music Room—usually cold and gloomy—glowed with unaccustomed light and color. There were decorations of bright autumn leaves everywhere and great numbers of lighted candles. On a special platform stood a large armchair for the guest of honor.

At the last moment Franz was too shy to make the speech of dedication, so Holzapfel took his place. He told Herr Lang that they were going to perform a symphony written by Franz Schubert in honor of the Herr Direktor's birthday and as a farewell to his school and comrades.

Schubert conducted the orchestra himself. This symphony was received with such enthusiastic applause that he was quite overcome; at the conclusion of the music he found himself, to his surprise and embarrassment, the center of a wildly cheering throng.

He had not suspected that he was so much loved and honored by both teachers and students at the Konvikt. It made his heart warm and happy, though he felt very sad at leaving all his friends.

While Franz was at St. Anna's he still continued his lessons with Salieri.

"But why," the Italian scolded, "must you always write quartets, symphonies, and songs? You waste your time. *Opera* is the only thing that counts. Think of Mozart and Gluck. How did they make fame, eh? *Opera!*"

Franz had always wanted to write a music-drama. But he knew little about this type of composition. He had never even heard an opera until Josef Spaun, soon after the move to St. Anna's, invited him to a performance of *The Swiss Family* (a then popular but long since vanished work) at the Royal *Hofoperhaus*.

Franz was enthralled by the opera. "Salieri is right!" he cried. "Opera *is* the thing—I must write one at once."

A few weeks later, when Spaun went to call on Franz at St. Anna's, he found him, as usual, in the midst of a pile of music manuscript. At first Schubert hardly noticed his friend, he was so absorbed in his work, and Spaun, well used to this kind of behavior, sat down to wait quietly.

Finally Franz looked up with a sigh of satisfaction. His face was flushed, and his short, brown curls stood up on end. He had a habit of running his fingers through his hair when he worked, as if he could stimulate his thoughts by tugging at the unruly locks.

"Josef," he said solemnly, "it is finished!"

"Good," Spaun replied, smiling. "What is it this time?"

For answer Schubert handed over a thick sheaf of closely written music sheets. On the first page was written: *Des Teufels Lustschloss.*

Spaun pursed up his lips in a whistle. "So-o-o! You have really written an opera—"

"A 'natural-magic opera'," Franz interrupted, rubbing his hands together. "Three hundred and forty-one pages long."

"And what a title! *The Devil's Pleasure Palace.* Where, Herr opera-composer, do you expect this masterpiece to be produced?"

Schubert's face clouded over. "Now you are mocking me, my friend. You know how difficult it is to get an opera produced."

"I was only teasing," Spaun broke in quickly. "But as a matter of fact you should have no difficulty. Salieri is sure to help you."

Franz himself was hopeful; had not the celebrated Italian urged him to write operas? Surely,

Signor Salieri would use his influence to assist his pupil.

But Schubert was doomed to disappointment: Salieri did nothing to help him, and *The Devil's Pleasure Palace* was never performed.

In August 1814 Franz finished his course at St. Anna's, and passed the examinations, not brilliantly, but well enough to be given a certificate as *Schulgehilf* or "school-assistant" for the primary grades. The records show that he was "good in spelling, knowledge of the alphabet, and pronunciation", "mediocre" in arithmetic and Latin, and "poor" in "practical religion".

On the day when he was to begin his duties as schoolmaster, Franz woke up with a dull sense of foreboding. Unconsciously he knew that something unpleasant was going to happen that day. Then he remembered. . . .

"Guten Morgen, Herr Schulgehilf!" Ferdinand cried, throwing back the covers of the big bed. Karl, on the other side, turned over with a groan and burrowed under the feather comforter for another nap. The three brothers were once again united in their little room under the eaves of the *Schwarzen Rössl.* Herr Schubert's wish was at last fulfilled: all four of his sons were now assisting him in the school.

Franz was usually the merriest of them all, in his quiet way, but this morning he was in no mood for joking. When Karl saw his despondency, he came over and put his arm across his youngest brother's shoulders. "Now don't take it so to heart, Franz!" he said kindly. "You don't have to give up *all* your music just because you are teaching school. Why, even I," he added wistfully, "find some time now and then for drawing and painting. And if the beastly youngsters get too wild, you know there's always the birch rod to make them listen to reason."

Frau Anna served a specially good breakfast that morning, with real coffee and cinnamon *Kaffee Küchen*. She looked sympathetically at Franz's gloomy face. Frau Schubert had not entirely approved of her husband's determination to turn his youngest son into a schoolteacher. After all, Franz did have unusual music talent; everyone at the Konvikt said so. He might have made the family famous if he had been allowed to continue with his composing. . . .

Herr Schubert had explained every detail of the new duties to his son, but when Franz found himself facing a roomful of wriggling, restless youngsters, all watching him with impish curiosity, he was seized with a panic greater than any he had ever felt before a music audience.

As youngest of the *Schulgehilfe*, Franz had been

given the least desirable of the crowded schoolrooms. It was small and low-ceilinged, and the windows opened on a dark, narrow court, so that even in fine weather the light was insufficient. During the winter months an oil lamp hung from the ceiling, smoky and evil-smelling, and it had to be kept burning most of the time. Rows of hard wooden benches and clumsy desks filled the room, and these were ink-stained and carved by the penknives of generations of restless students. The schoolmaster's table stood on a raised platform, and behind this a large blackboard hung on the wall.

"This is your new teacher—Herr Franz," Father Schubert told the children.

"*Guten Morgen, Herr Franz,*" they piped in dutiful chorus.

"Do not forget that you are to be obedient and studious," the headmaster said sternly, looking over the group with a critical eye; "especially you, Johann Müller, and you, Fritz Klein."

"Yes, sir," the pupils chorused again.

Then the moment that Franz had been dreading arrived. Herr Schubert left the room, and the new *Schulgehilf* was alone with his class. He felt as if he were paralyzed, his mind was a dreadful blank, and he didn't know what to say or where to begin.

A wave of mischief passed among the pupils. As plainly as if the words had been spoken, Franz imagined he could read their thoughts: "No need of being afraid of *this* teacher! He's a *Dummkopf*. He doesn't know anything. He can't control *us*—we can do exactly as we please."

The children grew more and more unruly, first in a tentative sort of way, as if to test the patience of the new teacher; then, as Franz still sat in frozen silence, they grew bolder, and began to run about and throw things at each other. Johann and Fritz were the ringleaders.

The new *Schulgehilf* was at his wits' end. He felt as if this were some dreadful nightmare in which he was powerless to speak or move. Then all at once, as the commotion threatened to bring down the roof, he remembered what Karl had said that morning: sure enough, there on the desk before him was the famous birch rod. Grasping it as a drowning man would cling to a straw, he rapped sharply.

"Silence!" he roared, suddenly finding his voice.

The children were so amazed that they stood petrified in their tracks.

"You, Johann Müller—and you, Fritz Klein. Come here to me and hold out your hands."

Order was finally restored, but Franz never knew how he managed to get through that awful morning. Each day thereafter was a new torment to his sensitive nerves; he wondered how he could possibly endure such an existence. Eventually, however, he made a discovery: by giving the children a difficult problem to work out, he could keep them quiet for a little while.

Then he would open the bottom drawer of his desk and, pulling out a sheet of ruled paper, place it between the covers of the lesson book and begin feverishly to write music. Minutes would pass unnoticed; suddenly Franz would become conscious that the classroom was no longer quiet. His pupils, having finished their problem, and aware that their teacher's attention was fixed on other things, would begin to amuse themselves.

Then all of Franz's lovely harmonies would vanish in thin air. Reluctantly he would come back from his world of music to the dark, noisy classroom. Automatically his hand would reach for the birch rod. "Silence!" he would roar, and continue with the lesson.

Franz's comrades from the Konvikt, Stadler and Holzapfel, came to see him shortly after he began his work at the Lichtenthal School. Father Schubert was not very enthusiastic over their visit; he did not care to have his son reminded of the musical career he had given up for teaching. Franz found there was no place in the crowded house where he could entertain his friends, and music was quite out of the question.

The two young men did not stay long. As they were leaving, Holzapfel drew Franz to one side. "You don't *know* how we miss your music, Franz!" he said. "Have you written many new things lately?"

Young Schubert shook his head sadly. "It is hard to write now. But I have a few songs. One to Mayrhofer's *Am See* is rather good, I think."

"We must hear it!" Stadler exclaimed. "Listen, Franz—there is no place here where you can make music. Why don't you come to the Konvikt once in a while?"

Franz welcomed the suggestion. Now, whenever he had a little free time on Sundays or holidays, he walked the long distance to the Konvikt to see his friends and have some music. Sometimes he would arrive just as they were leaving for church. Stadler, telling of this in later years, said:

If Schubert happened to be there at that time we used to lock him in the *Kamerade* (our living and studying room) and give him a few pieces of music-paper, and any volume of poems that happened to come to hand, so that he could pass the time. When we returned from church we generally found something ready which he would willingly present to some of us. . . . He brought to us faithfully what he composed at home, and we then hurried, with or without him, into one of the remotest rooms which had a pianoforte. He or I played, Holzapfel sang; we were full of admiration and ecstasy. They were beautiful times; noble enjoyments of youth! And when we thus gave vent to our feelings, he sat perfectly quiet at the instrument, smiled or told a joke. But all the while he was pleased that we had understood him.

CHAPTER VIII

Franz Falls in Love

"WELL, my boy, how goes it?" Herr Holzer cried, seizing Franz by both hands.

Schubert was walking down the street not far from the Lichtenthal church. He had not seen his old teacher for some time. Michael Holzer had been so indignant when Herr Schubert made a schoolteacher out of his youngest son that he refused to enter the house any more.

"How goes it?" Franz repeated gloomily. "As you can imagine!" A bitter note crept into his voice. "One of these days I shall probably go mad, and then they can no longer expect me to teach school."

Herr Holzer looked at the boy with compassion, but when he spoke his voice was sharp. "I did not expect this of you, Franz. Do you really intend to let life get the best of you?"

Schubert stared at the cobblestones under his feet. "What is the use of fighting against the inevitable?" he asked in a dull voice.

"You talk as if there were nothing left for you. That's stupid. A schoolmaster's assistant has plenty of spare hours which can be profitably used." He paused significantly, then added, "—by someone who is intelligent enough to take advantage of them."

"I don't know what the matter is," Franz exclaimed, sighing mournfully. "Music seems to have deserted me—"

Herr Holzer looked still more concerned. He shook his head and rubbed his red nose vigorously. This seemed to give him an inspiration.

"What you need is distraction, something to take your mind off yourself. Tomorrow evening there is to be music at the house of Frau Grob. She lives just across from the Lichtenthal church, you know. I have often spoken to her about you, and I am sure she would be delighted to have me bring you to her house."

Franz was only vaguely interested. Nothing seemed to matter much any more, but to please his old teacher he finally agreed.

Frau Grob and her young son and daughter lived in one of the finest houses in the Lichtenthal district. While life for the Schuberts had been a constant and bitter struggle, the Grobs had always enjoyed comfort and luxury. The two young people were both accomplished musicians; Heinrich played several different instruments, and sixteen-year-old Therese had an exceptionally beautiful voice; she could sing high D without difficulty.

Franz had often heard his teacher speak of the Grobs, but hardly expected that he would ever know them personally, for he was far below their level socially, and musically he was too unimportant to be invited to their home.

Because of the social prestige, Herr Schubert was pleased to have his son visit the Grobs. Franz, however, had no proper clothes, so Ferdinand offered to lend him his new black suit. It was only a little too long, and just a bit too snug in the middle; otherwise it fitted perfectly, and Franz was quite pleased when, face scoured and curls plastered down, he examined his reflection in the family mirror. He thought to himself, happily, that he was perhaps better-looking than he had feared. But he wished he were just a little taller, and didn't have to wear those awful spectacles!

When Herr Holzer and his former pupil arrived at Frau Grob's house there was already quite a crowd of people in the drawing-room. Franz, suddenly shy and uncomfortable in such elegant society, hid behind the portly figure of the old organist. His fine clothes did not seem quite so fine now in the midst of all these silks and satins.

Frau Grob was a handsome woman in her early forties; dressed in wine-colored taffeta with a fichu of lace and a cap to match, she was just seating herself as they arrived.

"We shall have to wait until later to greet our hostess," Herr Holzer said in a low voice. "The music is about to begin."

At that moment there was a stir at the door and a pompous, elegantly dressed little man strode into the room.

"It is Salieri," the people whispered.

Franz drew a little more into the shadow; he wondered what his teacher would think to find him there. Then the music began and he forgot everything else. First there was a string quartet, and next came one of Vienna's leading pianoforte players. Many celebrated musicians were heard at Frau Grob's musical soirées. The great Beethoven himself, so it was said, had once played at her house.

Franz, who had been starved for music, drank it all in like a thirsty plant. Just as he was wondering what would follow on the program, Salieri came forward leading Frau Grob's daughter by the hand. Therese was not a beautiful girl—rather plain and plump, and her fresh round face bore the scars of the dreaded smallpox. But Franz liked her frank countenance and simple, unaffected manner.

"Fräulein Therese is going to sing for us a song written by a young musician who is a pupil of mine," Signor Salieri announced. He peered around the room. "I believe that Herr Mayrhofer, who wrote the poem, is here this evening, and also, if I am not mistaken, the young man who composed the music."

Herr Holzer turned and nudged Franz, but the latter hardly noticed, he was so interested in trying to think who this pupil of Salieri's might be. Suddenly, to his surprise, he heard the opening bars of his own "*Am See*".

Was it possible that this was *his* song that Fräulein Therese was singing? Franz was quite overcome. The music sounded much more beautiful than he had imagined; Frau Grob's daughter not only had a fine voice, but she sang with unusual feeling and intelligence for a girl of sixteen.

The song was received with gratifying applause;

and Salieri, pleased by this success, dragged Franz from his corner (much against his will) to bow to the audience. Young Schubert would have died of embarrassment if he had not been so excited and so anxious to thank the charming Fräulein for her charming interpretation of his music.

"I did not know my song was so good," he told her shyly a little later. "But that is because you sing it so beautifully."

"I like your songs, Herr Schubert," Therese answered with straightforward sincerity. "They are delightful to sing. In fact, they seem to sing themselves!"

"Then I must write more for you," he rejoined quickly. "You have such a splendid voice. You should sing in opera. Now I have written an opera, *The Devil's Pleasure Palace*—"

"Oh, but Mother would never allow me to sing in public!" the little Fräulein exclaimed.

"Not even in church?" Franz, his bashfulness forgotten, felt as if he had stepped over into another world, where two congenial souls could meet in common and delightful understanding.

"Well, perhaps. That depends," Therese said, pursing her lips adorably. ("But she *is* pretty!" Franz thought, wondering how he could have considered her plain.)

"I have been writing a Mass," he went on, "for

the one-hundredth anniversary celebration at the
Lichtenthal church. If only *you* could sing the
soprano part!"

"But certainly the Signorina must sing the
soprano part!" a voice broke in behind them. Signor
Salieri was in a genial mood that evening. "I myself
shall persuade the good Frau Mama," he said, leading
Therese over to her mother.

As Franz stood, watching the graceful young
girl cross the drawing-room, he saw a tall, thin man
come towards him. The stranger wore dark clothes
and had such a melancholy expression that he would
have been noticeable in any gathering.

"Herr Schubert," the man said, holding out his
hand, "I wish to thank you for the fine setting you
have given my poem."

"*Your* poem?" Franz stammered. "Is it possible— Are you—?"

"Yes, Mayrhofer is my name."

"Oh, but, Herr Mayrhofer, it is I—it is *I* who
must thank you for writing such beautiful poetry."

The melancholy gentleman sighed. "Writing
poetry helps to pass the time," he said mournfully, "to
forget the sad reality of existence. But your music,
now, I find it well adapted to my poems. Perhaps
you would like to use some others for your songs?"

Franz assented eagerly.

"You must come and see me," Mayrhofer continued. "I should like to hear more of your music. Our friend Spaun shall bring you to my rooms. When can you come?"

Schubert's face lighted up. "Perhaps some Saturday afternoon? I do not have much free time."

Herr Holzer, from the other end of the room, watched Franz's shining eyes with satisfaction. Perhaps now the schoolroom would seem less terrible.

Schubert's Mass in F was performed on October 16, 1814, at the Lichtenthal church. He himself conducted, Herr Holzer played the organ and directed the choir, and Therese Grob sang the soprano part. The affair was such a success that the Mass had to be repeated ten days later in the Church of St. Augustine.

"Ah, yes," Salieri told his friends with a nonchalance that did not conceal his pride, "the young composer is one of my pupils. He could become great if his so stupid father did not make of him a *schoolteacher!*" The old Kapellmeister went on muttering in Italian something about "casting pearls before swine" and "Pegasus in harness".

As a matter of fact Herr Schubert was really proud of his son's success. "You see, Franz," he said firmly, "how right I was. Schoolteaching is not such a bad profession, after all. You have plenty of leisure for composition, but still it gives you an assured living and you don't have to depend on music for your daily bread."

Franz listened in respectful silence to his father, but he made no reply. He remembered how often the squirming children and the hated teaching had threatened to extinguish his inspiration forever.

Herr Schubert, to show his pleasure at his son's accomplishment, presented him with a small five-octave piano. This would have been an epoch-making event if Franz had not been completely absorbed at that time in his visits to the Grobs.

For now a real compensation had come into his life. In contrast to the dull, uninspiring, and depressing surroundings in his home and classroom, he found at the Grobs' an atmosphere that was congenial in every way. Frau Grob was a sympathetic person, and she understood the lonely boy's need for companionship and encouragement. Schubert was only seventeen at the time, but his genius and the hardships of his life had matured him at an early age, and he was already a man in his development.

Both Frau Grob and her children admired his music with sincere appreciation. Their house was open to him at any time he cared to come, and the

privilege of this friendship proved an inestimable influence in his life at that time.

Every moment that he could spare now was
given to the writing of music. He began work on
another symphony, and a string quartet in B flat was
composed in such a fury of inspiration that he completed the first movement in four hours and a half.
It was Schubert's habit—possibly inspired by his
father's painstaking exactness—to write on every score
the date on which it was begun, and that on which it
was completed, sometimes mentioning even the hour;
and because of this, later generations have been able
to learn definitely of the amazing swiftness with
which he wrote music. No one else but Mozart ever
had such facility in composition.

A few days after the performance of his first
Mass, while he was still in a state of rapture over
Fräulein Grob's beautiful singing, Franz wrote one
of his loveliest songs: "Gretchen at the Spinning-
Wheel," taken from Goethe's *Faust*. In this much-
loved song the murmur of the spinning-wheel runs in
soft accompaniment to the plaintive melody.

Fräulein Therese was so enthusiastic about
"Gretchen am Spinnrade" that Franz showed it to
Salieri.

"Ah, yes—a pretty little thing!" the Italian
commented. "Quite—ah, how do you say—ingen-
ious in its accompaniment. But as I tell you before,

songs they are—ah, only trifles. Leave poems alone, my boy, especially those of Goethe. Too many dunces, they try to set Herr Goethe to music."

Fortunately Franz did not take Salieri's advice too seriously. He could no more keep from writing songs than he could keep from breathing. Because music was his natural expression, whenever he heard a beautiful poem his mind would immediately translate the words into melody, and it was no more effort for him to put the music down on paper than for the average person to write a letter. Schubert composed over six hundred songs during his short lifetime, and seventy-three were to Goethe's poems! (Close to two hundred and fifty songs were written in the two years after he met Therese Grob.)

Franz went frequently to visit the Grobs; they treated him almost as one of the family. His music now was always included in their soirées, and often during his free hours he accompanied Therese on the piano when she was practising. At those times the bashful young schoolmaster could forget how sordid his everyday existence was and believe in a life where beauty only was reality.

It was perhaps inevitable that Franz should fall

in love with Therese. It did not matter to him that she was plain and pockmarked; her voice and her passion for music were far more important in his eyes than mere beauty. But he did not dare to tell her of his feelings, or even to admit them to himself. Who was he, the humble son of a struggling schoolmaster, to lose his heart to a wealthy, high-born Fräulein like Therese Grob?

One Sunday in June 1815, when the sun was out in unusual splendor, the Grobs decided to spend the day in the country and they invited Franz to go with them. Beyond the Wienerwald stretched open meadows bright with wild flowers and encircled by low-lying hills. Frau Grob's open victoria, drawn by the prancing pair of bay horses that were the admiration of the entire Lichtenthal district, took them to the edge of the woods, where they could sit in the shade of the trees and look out over the fields.

After they had eaten their lunch—a sumptuous repast served from a large wicker hamper, and very different from Frau Schubert's modest picnic-fare— Franz and Therese wandered out into the meadows together. Suddenly almost at their feet a lark rose into the air, and as it soared upwards it poured out a flood of silver melody. Therese was enraptured.

"How beautiful!" she cried. "Did you hear that song, Franz? How could any human being hope to sing as wonderfully as that!" She stared upwards

at the vanishing point of song. "And yet *your* music is just as moving."

"Do you think so?" Franz said eagerly. He reached timidly for his companion's hand, but Therese laughingly evaded him.

"The lark makes me think of the poem in Shakespeare's *Cymbeline*," she answered gaily. "Do you know it?"

Franz shook his head. He was not familiar with Shakespeare.

"'Hark! hark! the lark', it's called," Therese explained. "I wonder if I can remember it. . . ." She thought for a moment, and then the words came to her:

"Hark! hark! the lark at heaven's gate sings,
 And Phoebus 'gins arise,
His steeds to water at those springs
 On chaliced flowers that lies;
And winking Mary-buds begin
 To ope their golden eyes;
With everything that pretty bin,
 My lady sweet, arise!
  Arise, arise!"

"That's truly beautiful!" Franz exclaimed when Therese had finished. And he was not sure which he thought the lovelier—the poem, or the way she recited it. "Some day I shall write a song to those words," he continued. "You know, I can never hear poetry without wanting to set it to music. My friends tell me I don't know the difference between good and bad poems."

Therese laughed, and Franz thought her laughter sounded as melodious as the song of the lark that had just flown singing into the sky. "It wouldn't make much difference what the words were if *you* set them to music, my friend," the young girl said earnestly. "Any poem would become beautiful if you wrote a melody for it."

The floodgates of Franz's heart were opened. "Therese!" he cried. "My dear, dear friend, it is *you* who have inspired me. With your help I could always write beautiful music. I—" Suddenly, to his utter amazement, he found himself pouring out the words he had never even allowed himself to think. "I love you, Therese, I love you!"

The young girl was too startled to speak, and Franz, overcome by his audacity, began to stammer. "Of course, I shouldn't speak to you like this. Forgive me, Fräulein Therese."

His companion looked at him with candid eyes. "I think I love you, too, Franz," she said simply. "Your music moves me so deeply. But what would Mother think?" Therese sighed. "Unless you had a good position I'm afraid she would never allow me to marry you."

Franz came tumbling back to earth. "Of course

—I had forgotten. But, perhaps," his eyes lit up,
"perhaps I *could* find a musical position somewhere.
Or, if I didn't have to teach school, I might make
enough from my compositions to support a home. It
is so easy for me to write. Sometimes I do six, seven,
or even eight songs in a day; before I finish one,
another is begun. And the Mass, you know, was a
real success."

Therese tried to feel as hopeful as he, but she
knew too well what her mother's reaction would be.
"Perhaps we had better not mention it to Mother
just now," she said.

Nothing ever came of Franz's beautiful dream.
He tried very hard to secure a musical position. In
1816 he made application to the Government School
of Music at Laibach:

Most Honored Imperial Royal Town Governor:
The writer humbly implores you to grant him the vacant position as director of music at Laibach.

He gives the following grounds for his request:

1. He is a pupil of the Imperial and Royal Konvikt,
and has been an Imperial and Royal Chorister at Court; a
student in composition under Herr von Salieri, first Imperial
and Royal Court Kapellmeister, on whose well-meaning advice he applies for the vacant post.

2. In every branch of composition he has acquired such knowledge and ability in the playing of the organ, violin, and in singing, that according to the enclosed certificate he is declared to be the most capable among all the petitioners for this position.

3. He undertakes to use his abilities to their utmost extent and prove himself worthy if his request is graciously granted.

FRANZ SCHUBERT
Temporarily School Assistant at his
father's school in Vienna.

Himmelpfortgrund No. 10.

The directors, however, evidently felt that young Schubert was not experienced enough to hold such a responsible position, and his request was refused. During the next two years, whenever Franz heard of a musical post that was vacant he put in an application, but none of his efforts met with success, and he was obliged to continue in his hated profession of schoolteaching.

Five years later Therese married a wealthy banker much older than herself. Frau Grob arranged the match, and her daughter dutifully obeyed, though it was rumored that she was not happy in the choice. Franz never returned to the Grobs' house after the marriage.

No one but Holzapfel knew of Franz's unfortunate attachment for Therese. His other friends be-

lieved him to be immune to love. Years later Anselm
Hüttenbrenner wrote of a conversation he once had
with Schubert:

"During a country walk which I took with
Schubert in 1821 I asked him if he had ever been in
love. Because he showed himself to be so cold and
unresponsive towards the fair sex, I formed the opinion that he disliked women. 'Oh, no,' he replied. 'I
loved one with all my heart, and she loved me in return. She was somewhat younger than I, and she
sang the soprano solos magnificently and with deep
feeling in a Mass I composed. She was not beautiful,
and her face was marked with smallpox, but she was
good—good to the heart. For three years I hoped to
marry her, but I could find no situation, which caused
both of us great sorrow. She then married another
man, because her parent wished it. I still love her,
but since then no other can please me so well or better.
The fact is, she was not destined for me.' "

CHAPTER IX

The Erl-King

"ONLY two more flights now, Franzl!"
Josef Spaun called over his shoulder as
he and his friend climbed the long stairs
of the ancient building where Johann
Mayrhofer lived.

"*Donnerwetter!*" Franz replied, puffing vigorously. "If I weren't so anxious to meet that remarkable poet again I could never climb so far."

Spaun laughed heartily. "What you need is
more exercise! Look at your figure. . . ."

"*Exercise!* And when would I find time for exercise? Teaching those stupid children all day—
hardly any time left for writing music."

"Well, I must say you make the most of that time, my lad," his friend rejoined as he reached the top landing and knocked vigorously on Mayrhofer's door.   "Some new composition every day . . . I don't see how you do it!"

"Come in," a lugubrious voice called.   Spaun opened the door and the two young men entered the room.

Although the sun was still shining outside, it was almost dark in Mayrhofer's room.   The street was very narrow, and a tall building across the way shut off most of the light and kept the place in a perpetual twilight.   The ceiling was stained and bulging in places from the leaky roof above; the furniture was falling in pieces, and everything was in such a dingy, disordered, and dilapidated state that Franz wondered how anyone could live in such depressing surroundings.   (He would have been surprised to know that a few years later he would be glad to share these same quarters with his friend.)

Mayrhofer, a man ten years older than Schubert, was desperately poor.   But, strangely enough, that did not bother him; as long as he had a little money to buy tobacco, paper for his writing, and music, he was perfectly happy.   In one corner of the room stood a decrepit piano, and on the table lay an ancient guitar half covered with a litter of papers.

"I have been playing over some of your music,

Herr Schubert," he said with cordial welcome. "It is beautiful—really beautiful!" His large, deep-set blue eyes and melancholy face lit up with a singularly sweet smile. Franz, who had long admired Mayrhofer's poems, felt that he had found a kindred spirit.

Before long young Schubert was seated at the piano, playing snatches of songs, quartets, and dance music, and improvising new melodies as he went along. Mayrhofer leaned over the piano with unaffected delight, while Josef Spaun lounged in one of the battered chairs and closed his eyes the better to enjoy the music.

Then, as Franz played, Mayrhofer began to read his poems aloud. It would have been hard to say who was the more enthusiastic—Franz over Mayrhofer's poems, or the latter over young Schubert's music.

"We must do an opera together!" the poet finally exclaimed. Rapidly the plot was sketched out. . . . The hours passed, and darkness filled the room.

Only then did the two young men realize how late it had grown. As Spaun and Schubert prepared to leave, Mayrhofer had a sudden inspiration. "They are giving Gluck's *Iphigenia in Tauris* at the Opera this evening," he cried. "Why don't—" He broke off a moment to feel in his pocket; yes, he had just enough money left! "Why don't we all go together and hear the great Milder and Vogl?"

Franz felt a little guilty about his long absence from home. He hoped that Frau Mama would not worry. But after all, this was Saturday, and it was seldom enough that he could get away. And besides, was he not eighteen years old now, a man earning his own living?

No one thought of supper. By hurrying they were able to join the line standing in front of the opera in time to get seats in the gallery. Gluck, after Mozart, was Franz's favorite opera composer; the three young men were in a state of high excitement after the stimulating afternoon they had spent together, and they applauded the singers with such enthusiasm that everyone in the gallery turned to look at them.

Anna Milder, leading soprano of the Court Opera, was a great favorite with the Viennese people; but most popular of all the singers was Johann Vogl, who that evening sang the role of Orestes. He was a tall, romantic figure of a man, with the features of a Greek god, and a striking personality that fascinated all who knew him. Franz was carried away by Vogl's interpretation of Orestes.

When the performance came to an end, Spaun invited his two companions to have supper with him. "We will go to the *Blumenstöckl* [Flower-pot] for a Schnitzel and a glass of beer," he said.

Mayrhofer was singularly quiet. As they went

down the steps of the opera house he stumbled and would have fallen if Franz had not held him up. "What is it?" he and Spaun asked anxiously. "Are you ill?"

The poet drew himself up with a sheepish smile. "It's nothing—nothing!" he answered quickly. "Only that—well, I probably forgot to eat today. Silly habit of mine. . . ." He did not add that it was a habit Fate had forced upon him. Often Mayrhofer spent his last *pfennigs* for music instead of food. ("Music is much more sustaining than food!" he would insist.)

As the three young men entered the coffee-house, Spaun found a group of his friends there who had also just come from the opera: Josef and Anselm Hüttenbrenner and Franz von Schober.

Schober was the son of a Viennese mother and Swedish father. Brought up in Scandinavia, he had recently come to Vienna to complete his studies at the University, and had rapidly become popular in the gayest social circles of the city. He was brilliant, merry, and light-hearted, with a great deal of personal charm and magnetism. Yet in spite of his frivolous disposition, Schober had a genuine love for music. He had long wanted to meet Franz Schubert, so when Spaun suggested that they all join together and sit at one table, he agreed with enthusiasm.

Franz fell completely under the spell of Schober (who eventually became his closest friend), but he was less impressed at first with the Hüttenbrenner brothers.   Later, however, when Schubert discovered that both Anselm and Josef were ardent admirers of his music, a warm friendship began that lasted until the end of his days.

The young men, that evening at the "Flower-pot", were all full of praise for the opera and singers they had just heard.   "Frau Milder is not bad-looking," Schober said, with the air of a connoisseur.

"And what a voice!" declared Mayrhofer.

"Nothing on earth could be more beautiful than her singing," Franz cried with enthusiasm.   "Frau Milder's voice goes straight to one's heart.   And as for Herr Vogl. . . ."   Franz was so excited that he forgot his usual silent role.   "Herr Vogl was so magnificent that I should like to fall at his feet and thank him for the joy he has given me!"

At a neighboring table a glum-looking University Professor sniffed in audible contempt.   "Frau Milder has a voice like a rooster," he said sourly; "she doesn't know how to sing, and that conceited Vogl with his elephant feet—"

Schubert and young Schober jumped up in a passion of resentment.   Franz knocked over his glass of beer in his indignation, and for a moment it looked as if the *Blumenstöckl* would be the scene of a hand-to-hand, knockdown fight.   But Spaun and Mayrhofer separated the belligerents.

"After all," Spaun said soothingly, "everyone has a right to his own opinions.   And if—" he bowed ceremoniously to the University Professor—"if our esteemed friend here is lacking in taste, it is hardly our duty to try to improve it."

The Professor gathered his hat and papers together, glared at the six young enthusiasts, bowed stiffly from the waist and made his departure.

By now it was very late.   Franz wondered if he would be able to rout out anyone at his father's house to let him in.

"You shall come home with me, my Franzl," Spaun insisted.   "Tomorrow is Sunday—no classes for you, and I have an extra couch, you know."

This was an evening often repeated in future months.   Josef Spaun wrote in his later memoirs:

He [Schubert] accepted unhesitatingly the offer of a friend [Spaun himself] to share for many years the jovial supper which usually lasted till after midnight.   When it became very late he did not go home, but contented himself with a modest accommodation in my room, where he often slept without taking off his spectacles, to which he was so much accustomed.   In the morning he would sit down at the table clad only in his shirt and pants, and compose the most beautiful things, mostly songs, and sometimes also the most lovely German dances and Ecossaises which were then the fashion for us dance-loving couples. . . . Schubert himself never danced. . . .

Schubert's daily life, teaching the unruly youngsters at his father's school, continued to be a martyrdom for him. How could he concentrate on stupid lessons in reading and arithmetic when his head was always filled with bright melodies that clamored to be put down on paper before they disappeared forever! Just as he would be about to write out a problem on the blackboard, or hear the stumbling recital of a memorized poem, some specially lovely theme would come lilting from the skies. Franz's eyes would take on a faraway look. . . .

"Children, you may have a few minutes to prepare for the next lesson," he would announce, reaching for his music-paper. But it was seldom that he had time enough to capture the fleeting inspiration.

At least now he could look forward to certain hours of companionship with friends who shared his interest and were always ready to applaud the music he brought them.

Spaun and Mayrhofer, Stadler and Senn from Konvikt days, and now Schober and the Hüttenbrenners, met regularly each Saturday with him at the *Blumenstöckl*, or in Spaun's or Mayrhofer's rooms. This was the beginning of a "circle"—the "Schubertians" they called themselves.

As the years went on, this group came to include a large number of Schubert's devoted friends and admirers, and was the one great compensation in his otherwise tragic existence. The enthusiasm of these friends sustained his spirit and proved the inspiration for much of his music.

Although Franz still had to spend most of his time teaching school, the year 1815 (when he was only eighteen years old and in love with Therese Grob) proved one of the richest in composition of his entire life. During these months he wrote a third symphony, two Masses, quantities of other music for the Church, five operettas with texts by Mayrhofer, many piano compositions, a number of string quartets, and, most important of all, one hundred and forty-four songs.

Each composer is remembered for some especial form which is his particular contribution to music. Haydn brought the symphony form to perfection, Beethoven's "Scherzos" were new in his day, while Schubert's great legacy was the song. No one before or since his time has written such a large number of completely charming and melodious songs. They flowed from his pen as if some higher power were pouring down music from another sphere.

Sometimes he was seized with such a frenzy of inspiration that he would be beside himself until the impulse was captured. *"Rastlose Liebe"* ("Restless Love") came to him in this way, in 1815, and also the delightful *"Heidenröslein"* ("Hedge Rose"). Here are its words:

HEIDENRÖSLEIN

Words by Goethe, translated by Charles Fonteyn Manney

Once a boy a rose espied,
  In the hedgerow blooming;
Fresh and young, the morning's pride,
Thinking not her charms to hide,
  All the air perfuming.
    Little wild rose, wild rose red,
    In the hedgerow blooming.

Said the boy, "I'll gather thee,
  In the hedgerow blooming."
Said the rose, "My thorns you'll see,
Painful will the ending be
  Of your rash presuming."
    Little wild rose, wild rose red,
    In the hedgerow blooming.

Undismayed, he plucked the rose
  In the hedgerow blooming,

Vainly she laments her woes,
Vainly doth her thorns oppose,
Gone her sweet perfuming.
Little wild rose, wild rose red,
In the hedgerow blooming.

One Saturday afternoon towards the end of the year, Franz failed to come as was his custom to join the "Schubertians" at the tavern. Spaun finally went over to the *Schwarzen Rössl* to find out what had happened to his friend. He found Schubert pacing up and down the deserted schoolroom, a book in his hand, and a familiar, faraway look in his eyes.

"Listen!" he cried when Spaun opened the door. "This is magnificent . . . a poem by Goethe. It stirs your very blood!" In a voice trembling with emotion he began to read:

DER ERLKÖNIG

By Goethe, translated from the original German

Who rides through the night in tempest wild?
It is a father with his child;
He holds the boy safe in his arm,
He guards and shields him from all harm.

FATHER: "My son, why hid'st thou thy sweet face?"
SON: "See'st, father, thou the Erl-King? Alas!
The dreaded Erl-King, with crown and
    plumes?"
FATHER: "My son, 'tis a shape the mist assumes."

ERL-KING: "Thou lovely child, come thou with me!
I'll pass the hours in playing with thee,
The sweetest blossoms for thee shall grow,
And glittering raiment to thee I'll show."

SON: "My father, my father, and dost thou not hear
What Erl-King whispers into mine ear?"
FATHER: "Be silent, oh, be silent, my child;
Through bared branches the storm moans wild."

ERL-KING: "Thou dear sweet child, wilt come with me
Where wondrous games I'll play with thee?
Where their nightly revels my daughters keep
And swaying and dancing shall sing thee to
sleep."

SON: "My father, my father, look! yonder I see
The Erl-King's daughters on darksome lea!"
FATHER: "My son, my son, I see it well—
The old willow trees their secrets tell."

ERL-KING: "I love thee, child—thy beauteous form;
Art thou not willing, I'll take thee by storm!"
SON: "My father, my father, he now holds me fast,
Erl-King has seized me now—at last!"

The father trembles, he rides on, wild,
He clasps to his bosom the weeping child;
He reaches home in fear and dread;
Alas, in his arms the child was dead!

"Can't you hear the distracted father—the wild
voice of the Erl-King—the clatter of the horse's
hoofs?" Franz cried in excitement.

He threw himself into the chair by his desk and began to write feverishly. Spaun, who had often witnessed just such creative spells, did not interrupt his friend, but sat quietly on one of the school benches, and took out a book of Marcus Aurelius that he always kept in his coat pocket.

Nothing could be heard in the silent schoolroom but the furious scratching of Franz's pen and occasional snatches of melody as he hummed some of the parts while he went along. Then suddenly:

"It's done!" He held up the paper and waved it triumphantly. "Josef—" Schubert's voice was solemn—"this is one of the best things I've ever written." He looked around the schoolroom. "There is no place here where I can play it for you. Let's go over to the Konvikt."

On their way to the Konvikt they met Schober, and one or two others joined them. Ruziczka, the old Court organist and director of music at Herr Lang's school, was just coming down the steps as the band arrived.

"Franz has composed a new song, Herr Musik-direktor," they cried. "Come back with us to hear it."

Ruziczka took a fatherly interest in his former pupil's compositions, so he willingly turned back and went with them to the Music Room. He spread out the manuscript pages on the piano, and himself played

the new song through.   First comes the galloping of
the horse:

And then the story of the terrible ride begins:

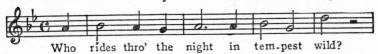

Who   rides thro' the   night   in   tem-pest   wild?

When Ruziczka had finished, there was a breath-
less silence.

"*Kolossal!*" Schober exclaimed in an awed voice.
"Magnificent!" cried Spaun with enthusiasm.   "But
those discords, now—do you think the public will like
that?"

Ruziczka turned on the speaker indignantly.
"But that is exactly where the genius comes in.   Here
—" he illustrated on the piano—"do you not see how
the dramatic quality is emphasized by the dissonance,

where the child cries to his father?   And here again
. . . Franz," the old teacher's voice was filled with
emotion, "you have richly fulfilled your early promise.   I salute in you a great composer!"

The *"Erlkönig"*, however, in spite of the excitement which its first performance caused, was not
given publicly until four years later—on January 25,
1821.   We shall see later how that came about.

CHAPTER X

Freedom—at Any Price!

"GRÜSS GOTT!" Schubert said dully, looking up from his desk in the empty schoolroom. "Oh, it's you, Josef!" He groaned, miserably. "I've been trying to write some German dances for Schober, but the ideas simply won't come."

Spaun smiled at his young friend with sympathetic affection. "What you need is a change of air, Franz," he said, taking him by the arm. "Come with me."

Josef Spaun had just moved out into the Erdberg district on the outskirts of Vienna. He had rooms there in the house of a Professor Watteroth; it was a pleasant location, with a garden full of flowers and shady trees. When he and Schubert reached the place, he took his friend into a sunny room overlooking the garden.

"Now then, my lad, here is a place where you can work!"

Franz stood in the middle of the floor, not quite understanding what his friend meant.

"This room shall be yours, Franz, as much as it is mine. You can come here whenever you need to escape—whenever you want to write undisturbed." He closed the door softly, and Schubert heard the click of the lock.

"You are a prisoner now," Spaun called through the keyhole. "And the price of your release is a new German dance."

Franz looked around the sunny, quiet room with a sigh of satisfaction. No noisy children here to distract him, no family coming in with constant interruptions. On the table was a pile of fresh music-paper, and beside it stood an inkstand and two new quill pens. Chuckling to himself, he pulled up a chair and began to write.

When Spaun released him a few hours later, Franz handed him not one, but twelve short German dances, and six *Ecossaises* besides. On the title page was written:

While prisoner in my room in Erdberg. 1 May, 1816. *Gott sey Lob und Dank.* [God be praised and thanked.]

Professor Watteroth and his family occupied the ground floor of the house where Spaun had his rooms. The Professor was a man of fine intellect, devoted to all the arts, and especially to music. Each week he gave an informal concert in his spacious drawing-room, and anyone who loved music was made welcome. The "Schubertians" were received with open arms, and Franz's songs and chamber music came to be the favorite entertainment.

A few weeks after Schubert's first introduction to the Watteroths, the Professor waylaid the young composer as he was going up to visit Spaun.

"On my name-day we usually have a special program of music in the garden," he told him. "Now I wonder if you would care to compose something for this year's celebration?"

Franz was, of course, delighted at the opportunity.

"A cantata, perhaps?" the Professor suggested. "This poem of *Prometheus* by Dräxler would make a good libretto. And would one hundred florins * be a satisfactory fee?"

Schubert swallowed quickly. "Quite satisfactory, Herr Professor," he replied.

One hundred florins! This was the first money Franz had ever earned from his music, and it seemed to him a princely sum. He set to work on the cantata

* About $20 in our money today.

at once and, according to the notation on the score, completed the work in a day:

June 17, 1816. On this day I composed for the first time for money. To wit, a Cantata, for the Name-day cele-bration of Professor Watteroth, by Dräxler. The fee is 100 florins.

Because of bad weather the concert had to be postponed, but finally on July 24 a large group of friends and neighbors assembled in the Watteroths' garden, and *Prometheus* was given with great success. Professor Watteroth and his family all took part, and a number of the "Schubertians" joined in the chorus.

Leopold Sonnleithner, an old friend of Konvikt days, was in the audience, and he was so enthusiastic about *Prometheus* that he arranged to have it per-formed at his father's house three years later. It was not given publicly, however, until 1828, shortly be-fore Schubert's death. Following this the manuscript disappeared.

The success of *Prometheus*, and especially the money that it brought him, made Franz believe for a short time that he was on the road to success. But then followed months of discouragement. No fur-ther orders came in, the publishers would not take his work, and the chains that bound him to the school-room seemed stronger than ever.

"A man bears misfortune without complaining, and finds it thereby the harder to bear," wrote Schubert in his diary on September 16, 1816. "Why, then, did God endow us with sympathy?"

One day Franz von Schober, gay and debonair, came in towards the close of Schubert's class to carry his friend off to a meeting of the "circle".

The children were in an uproar. Franz had never been a good disciplinarian; either he was over-strict, irritable, and even sometimes unjust in punishing the young urchins, or else, lost in his own reveries he would let them do exactly as they pleased. Now they had got completely out of hand, and he was at his wits' end to know how to manage the situation.

"How can you stand this?" Schober asked, as the last noisy youngster departed with slate and schoolbooks under his arm.

Franz groaned. "I don't know. I *can't* stand it, as a matter of fact. . . ."

"Then why don't you give up teaching school?" Schober insisted.

"For the simple reason," Franz answered grimly, "that I like to eat!"

His friend laughed. "Don't be foolish. With the reputation you are getting from your compositions you should be able to support yourself by writing music."

"I wish I could believe that!" Franz replied doubtfully. He looked around the hated schoolroom, at the stained desks and worn wooden floor, at the gloomy view into the courtyard outside the window, and at the smoking lamp that hung from the low ceiling. Suddenly he stood up and shook his fist violently. "But I don't care if I do starve. You are right—*anything* would be better than this!"

Schober put his arm across the young musician's shoulders. "Your friends won't let you starve, my Franzl, and you are welcome to share my rooms until you find a better lodging-place."

Franz had a difficult time telling his father what he had decided. But to his surprise, Herr Schubert accepted the news philosophically. Perhaps he had finally realized that "neither God nor man" could make a schoolteacher out of his youngest son. Nevertheless Father Schubert made it quite clear that he was in no position to help Franz financially. "You will have to look after yourself now," he said. "I have done what I could. . . ."

Franz's rebellion against schoolteaching proved contagious. Karl, next to him in the family circle, had also been forced into the profession by his father against his will, and he hated it almost as much as did his youngest brother. Now Karl decided that he too would follow his heart's desire, and devote himself to art. Before his death Karl Schubert became a landscape painter of considerable renown.

Frau Anna was secretly pleased with Franz's decision to devote himself to music.

"I know you will succeed," she said kindly. "And don't worry too much about your finances." She drew him to one side. "Whenever there is a little extra money in the house, I always tuck it away in this old gray stocking. As long as there is anything there you shall not go hungry!"

Franz was sincerely touched at his stepmother's kindness. More than once in years to come the gray stocking helped to tide him over a difficult period. As a last resort he would turn—not to his father—but to the one who had faith in him.

"Anything in the stocking, Frau Mama?" he would ask.

And Anna Schubert invariably found something to share with her youngest stepson.

Franz felt as free as the air when for the last time he shook the dust of the schoolroom from his feet. He was almost penniless, for during his years of teaching there had seldom been much left over from his meager salary—after he had paid his father for his board!—but this did not disturb Franz. His new friend Schober had invited him to share his rooms, and Schubert hoped that now at last he would begin to make a little money from his compositions.

Each morning he wakened with a fresh sense of release. No school!—no hated children to teach! Nothing to do but write music all day, and that was pleasure, not *work*. But he soon found that his time was not quite so free as he had hoped.

Schober, although sincerely devoted to music, lived only for pleasure. He was constantly dragging Schubert out to parties, and to long evenings at the coffee-houses and taverns, where there was too much of everything—wine, laughter, and conversation. It was usually far into the night before Schober could be persuaded to return to his rooms.

Franz discovered that the only undisturbed time he could find was early in the morning, while his friend was still sleeping. So he would rise at dawn, sit down at once, and begin his writing. New compositions continued to flow in a stream, but it seemed impossible to interest the publishers in his work.

One morning, when Josef Spaun came in, Franz put his music paper to one side and asked his friend to sit down.

"I must talk to you, Josef," he said, closing the door into the room where Schober lay sleeping.

"This can't go on," he continued dismally; "I simply won't be a burden on my friends forever."

Spaun started to remonstrate, but Franz went on quickly: "I keep taking my music to the publishers, and they always answer the same thing: 'Yes, that's very pretty, but you understand our position, Herr Schubert: we can't afford to risk our money on an unknown composer's work.'"

"Blind, stupid fools!" Spaun snorted. "The Viennese publishers are all a short-sighted, hardheaded lot. Now I have heard that Breitkopf and Härtel in Dresden are much more liberal-minded towards new composers. Why don't you send them a copy of the 'Erlkönig'?"

"That's not a bad idea," Franz said thoughtfully. He immediately made out a fresh copy of his song and sent it to the Dresden publishers.

As it happened, there was in Dresden another composer also named Franz Schubert, the director of the Italian opera there; and Breitkopf and Härtel suspected that someone was trying to play a hoax on them. They therefore sent the manuscript of "The Erl-King" to the Dresden Schubert, asking what he knew about the song.

That worthy gentleman was highly indignant. "This is an outrage," he cried. "I never composed a cantata on the 'Erlkönig', and you may be sure that I shall try to find out who sent this patchwork to you.

I should like to know who has stolen my good name for such base purposes!" How surprised he would have been if anybody had told him that his sole claim to immortality was to be this accidental association with the man who had composed "this patchwork"!

As for its real composer, Franz Peter Schubert, he never even had a reply from Breitkopf.

"But, Herr Vogl," Schober insisted, "I assure you Franz Schubert is really a very remarkable composer. . . ."

The celebrated baritone of the Vienna Opera looked around the roomful of elegantly dressed people with a bored expression. "No doubt this Herr Schubert is all that you say," he replied. "But so many young musicians are recommended to me. And nothing ever comes of them!"

Johann Vogl, although now close to fifty, was still a "figure of romance". Unusually tall and strikingly handsome, he was idolized by society, yet himself had no interest in social affairs. He was by nature a student and a mystic, and his spare hours—even during his off-stage moments at the Opera—were spent with religious and philosophical works, or in translating the Greek and Latin classics. Schober had met the extraordinary Vogl at a number of social functions, and had spoken to him several times of the promising young composer. But it was hard to interest the singer.

When Schober reported Vogl's remarks to Franz, the latter sadly replied: "I did not really expect anything else. Why should Herr Vogl care to meet such an unimportant person as myself?"

But one day Schober persuaded the opera singer to come and have just a look at his friend's songs.

When Vogl came in, rather pompous and condescending, he was so tall that he almost filled the little room. And Franz, who was only an inch over five feet in height, and was, besides, quite overcome by the unexpected honor of the visit, appeared even smaller and more insignificant than usual.

"I understand that you have written some songs," Vogl remarked. "Let me see what you have."

Franz was so paralyzed with timidity that he could neither move nor speak, but Schober handed the singer a pile of manuscript music. Vogl looked them over, humming an occasional phrase that caught his fancy.

"Not bad!" he said with lofty approval. Then he came upon the *"Erlkönig"*. "What's this, now?" He studied the score with growing interest. "But this is *good!* Play it through for me, will you, Herr Schubert?"

As soon as Franz sat down at the piano he forgot his self-consciousness. Vogl too became so interested that he set aside his role of condescending patron and interpreted the song with dramatic enthusiasm.

Something rare was born at that moment: here was the meeting of two great artists—one creator, and the other interpreter. It was a perfect combination, destined to continue through many years. The two traveled together on several occasions, giving concerts as they went—with Franz accompanying and Vogl singing the young composer's songs. Wherever they appeared together they made an unforgettable impression. Schubert wrote in a letter:

"The way in which Vogl sings and I accompany him, so that we seem to be fused for the moment into a single being, is something new and unknown to these people."

At their first meeting, however, Vogl had not yet reached the enthusiasm he was soon to feel for Schubert's music. As the singer was about to leave, he turned to Franz with a touch of his grand manner. "There is something in you," he admitted, "but you are not enough of a comedian, too little of a charlatan. You waste your beautiful thoughts without making the most of them."

Schubert's songs haunted the opera singer, and it was not long before he returned to hear more of this music. Soon Vogl became one of Franz's greatest admirers. Whenever he sang, the ladies would crowd around him, fascinated by his voice and appearance, and by the lovely new songs he sang. Franz, sitting quietly in a corner, would usually be completely ignored. But the modest young composer did not mind—he would have been terribly embarrassed if anyone had noticed him!

By the time he was twenty years old, Schubert had already composed over five hundred different works, and not one of these had appeared in print. The year 1817 saw the completion of the Sixth Symphony (the Fourth, called the *Tragic*, and the lovely Fifth in B flat had both been written the year before) and sixty-seven other compositions, including two overtures "in the Italian style".

Rossini had recently come to Vienna, and his operas—especially the famous *Barber of Seville*—had been received there with tremendous acclaim. Franz liked the Italian's operas, but he was a little scornful of their simple musical construction. "Anyone can write music like that!" he exclaimed, and just to show how easy it was to compose "in the Italian style", he immediately dashed off an overture similar to the one he had just heard.

Ironically enough, Schubert's first composition to be performed in public (with the exception of some church music) was an overture "written in the style of the old Italian school". On the evening of March 1, 1818, a "Musical Declamatory Academy" was held in the public-room of the inn *Zum römischen Kaiser*. ("Academy" was the old Austrian term for a miscellaneous concert or entertainment.) Franz felt that he had really "arrived" when he saw the announcement in the program: *"Italian Overture,* by Franz Schubert".

The work was well received, and the Viennese newspapers said:

The second part began with the loveliest overture by a young composer, Franz Schubert, a pupil of the famous Salieri. He understands how to touch and move the emotion of all hearts. Although the theme is simple enough, it contains an astonishing wealth of pleasant thoughts.

In 1818 also came the first appearance in print of Schubert's music. Two songs, composed to words by Mayrhofer, received immediate approval. They appeared in a specially prepared volume called "Picturesque Pocket Edition for Friends of the More Interesting Surroundings and Natural Wonders of the Austrian Monarchy."

The *Mourning* Waltz—*Trauerwalz* (so named by Schubert's publisher and for some time attributed to Beethoven)—was much admired by Schubert's

friends. When Anselm Hüttenbrenner asked him for
a copy, Franz, who was in high good humor over his
recent successes, wrote on the margin:

"Written for my dear Coffee, Wine, and Punch
brother, Anselm Hüttenbrenner, world-famous composer, Vienna, March 14, A.D. 1818, in his own imperial apartment, thirty florins monthly, Viennese
currency."

Another dedication of the same waltz was written in purposely bad Latin:

Illistrissimo, doctissimo, sapentissimo, prudentissimo,
maximoque, Compositori in devotissima, humilliumaque,
reverentiae expressione dedicatum oblatumque di Servorum
Servo Francisco Seraphico vulgo Schubert nominato.

Schubert cared little what happened to his music
after it was written down, and he was notoriously
careless with his manuscripts. If a friend asked him
for a piece of music he would shortly be given either
a specially composed work, or whatever came to
hand, and Franz seldom knew what became of these
afterwards. As a result, many of his manuscripts
were lost or mislaid.

Josef Hüttenbrenner later tried to recover the
countless stray scores that circulated around Vienna,
and it is thanks to his efforts that much of Schubert's
music was rescued from oblivion.

To this friend Franz dedicated one of his most

charming songs: "The Trout" (*"Die Forelle"*).   In the early eighteenth century blotters were unknown, and it was the custom to sprinkle sand over freshly written pages to dry the ink.   *"Die Forelle"* was written late at night, and the young composer was so sleepy that, instead of sand, he poured ink over the manuscript.   At the bottom of the score he wrote:

"Dearest friend, I am extremely glad that you like my songs.   As proof of my most devoted friendship I am sending you one which I have just composed at midnight whilst staying with Anselm Hüttenbrenner.   I wish I were in touch with you with a glass of punch.   By a stroke of bad luck, just as I intended to strew sand over this thing I was in a hurry, and, being very sleepy, picked up the inkstand, and poured it all unthinking over the manuscript.   *Vale!*"

CHAPTER XI

Count Esterházy and His Family

SCHUBERT was now beginning to receive considerable public recognition, but he was still desperately poor. He could not even make enough from his music for the barest necessities of life—which were all that his simple nature required. And now Franz von Schober, on whom he depended so much, was about to leave Vienna for a visit to Sweden.

"If you could only find some wealthy patron," Schober said, "some rich amateur who can afford to pay for the privilege of indulging his musical fancy, then you would no longer need to worry."

Franz shook his head. "I could not bear to be dependent on a stranger," he answered.

"Some of the greatest composers have welcomed such an opportunity!" his friend rejoined. "Take Haydn, for instance. Think of the years he lived as music-director in the household of Prince Esterházy. And even your idol Beethoven did not disdain the help of Prince Lichnowsky. It just means dedicating a few compositions, playing music for them now and then, and perhaps giving a few lessons."

Franz groaned. "Music-lessons! It's even worse to teach music than to teach school. I tried giving piano lessons to some of the elegant young Fräuleins whom Professor Watteroth sent to me, you know. But I had to give it up."

Schober loved his friend too much to reply, "Beggars must not be choosers," but he began to inquire around Vienna, hoping to hear of some rich nobleman who would be interested in a promising, if unknown, young composer.

It happened that a certain Count Esterházy (distant relative of the Prince who had been patron to Haydn) was just then looking for someone to spend the summer with his family at Zelész, the Esterházys' country estate in northern Hungary. The Count and his wife, the Countess Rosine, both loved music; they had good voices and enjoyed singing together, and they wanted a young man who could make music with them, and give piano lessons to their two small daughters.

There were many advantages in this position: it meant escape from the summer heat in Vienna, a pleasant outing in the country with free board and lodging, and, not least important, a certain remuneration for the lessons—to be paid for at two gulden each (about forty cents). Schubert applied for the place and, through the recommendation of Salieri and other friends, was accepted.

In July the Esterházys moved to the country, and Franz went with them. Zelész lay near the border between Hungary and Slovakia*—actually not far distant from Vienna; but this was the longest

* Until 1806, the country into which Schubert was born was called "The Empire"—a vast, straggling mass of different peoples, loosely united under "The Emperor". This "Empire" went out of existence in 1806 when Napoleon took Vienna; and after his fall in 1815 there was a general rearrangement of Central Europe. A large part of what had been the Empire persisted under the name Austria-Hungary, and its ruler was still sovereign over many different peoples—not only the Austrians and the Hungarians, but also the southern Slavs (who were later to form Yugoslavia), the Czechs, Moravians, and others (who were later to form Czechoslovakia), a corner of Poland, and bits of what was later to be Rumanian territory. This country of Austria-Hungary lasted until the First World War split it up, many of its subject peoples becoming independent—briefly.

journey Schubert had ever taken. He was tremendously excited, though he sat so quietly in his corner of the coach that no one would have suspected how much everything interested him. The new country through which they passed, the wayside inns where the horses were changed, the appearance of his fellow-passengers, were to him all part of a fascinating adventure.

But as usual, the sounds of the journey made the deepest impression of all; he was acutely conscious of the creaking wheels, the cries of the coachman, and the monotonous clatter of the horses' feet. These suggested new themes and rhythms to young Schubert's music-saturated consciousness, and he frequently jotted them down in a little notebook he always carried in his pocket. He was distressed because the jolting and swaying of the coach made it impossible to do any real writing.

At first everything at Zelész pleased Franz. He was not even disturbed to find that he had been given a room in the bailiff's house and was expected to eat with the servants. The Count maintained quite an establishment at his country estate.

The evening after his arrival in Zelész, Franz had just gone to his room after supper when he heard a knock at the door. On opening it he found Count Esterházy's personal servant.

"Herr Schubert," the valet said, standing very straight, and looking haughtily down on the small young man with the spectacles, "my master desires your presence for music in the drawing-room."

Franz, who was not quite sure just what his social standing was in this household (he suspected that he stood a little above the cook, but not quite so high as the valet), answered quietly: "Very well, I will come at once."

The candles in the drawing-room were lighted when Franz arrived, and the Countess was seated at the piano with one of her small daughters on either side. Maria was thirteen years old, shy and plain, but Karola, younger by two years, already gave promise of becoming a great beauty.

"It is our custom to have a little music each evening, Herr Schubert," the Count explained gruffly. He had none of the exaggerated politeness usual in titled society.

Countess Rosine, on the contrary, possessed all the graces of her position. She swept to her feet. "Indeed I shall be glad to have someone relieve me of the accompanying," she said, with a condescending nod in Schubert's direction. "Often some of the neighbors drop in, and when our cousin Baron Schönstein arrives, we shall have some real singing."

Count Esterházy sang bass, and his wife was a

fair contralto; but when Franz heard the little Countess Maria he was visibly impressed.

"Your daughter has a very fine soprano voice," he told the mother. "She should be given the best instruction."

Little Karola edged closer. "But *I* can play the piano," she said eagerly. "It is more difficult to play the piano than to sing!"

Franz looked at the child with a quizzical expression. "Then you will have to work very hard," he exclaimed.

Schubert played for the Esterházys, and then they all sang together—Mozart and Haydn, and, to Franz's delight, a quartet by his friend Anselm Hüttenbrenner, which he found on the piano.

"And have *you* perhaps written some songs, Herr Schubert?" the Count asked.

Franz admitted modestly that he had written a few (he failed to add that actually he had already composed several hundred songs), and then proceeded to play a number through for them.

"But these are charming—delightful!" Countess Rosine exclaimed. "Bring us the words when you come over tomorrow, so we can sing them with you."

"If your gracious Ladyship will choose one of her favorite poems, I shall be glad to write a new song to bring tomorrow evening," said Franz. "Or if you prefer, there is one that I almost finished today—written to my friend Mayrhofer's *Einsamkeit* (loneliness)." Schubert was not always pleased with his work, but he felt that *"Einsamkeit"* was one of the best things he had written.

When the Esterházys' cousin, Baron Schönstein, arrived, Franz was delighted to find in him a real musician. The young nobleman had a very fine baritone voice, and was, besides, a true artist. When he sang he forgot himself in the music, and interpreted the songs with such sensitive understanding that his listeners were carried away. He would have been highly successful as a professional singer if he had cared to take up such a career.

Before Karl Schönstein met Schubert he was interested only in the music of the Italians; but on hearing Franz's songs he became so enthusiastic over them that from that moment he devoted himself exclusively to the young Viennese composer's music. In later years, when Vogl was no longer able to sing, Schönstein became the greatest of all Schubert's interpreters. He was even said to have drawn tears from Liszt's eyes when many years later he sang some of Franz's songs for this great master.

Karl Schönstein was only a year older than Franz, and the two young men soon became good friends. They roamed the countryside around Zelész together, and Karl introduced Schubert to the stirring music of Hungary.*

Wherever they went they seemed to find music. Fiddlers at the inns, playing spirited dance music; gypsy camps where there was always a violin or accordion wailing mournful Slavic melodies; and even at the castle the servants would sing at their work, while Franz lingered to catch the haunting folk tunes. The strange melancholy of this music stirred him deeply.

Schubert always carried his little notebook with him, and jotted down the tunes and rhythms that caught his fancy. A number of these later found their way into his piano music—*Impromptus, Moments Musicaux*, and sonatas—and especially in his dance music. Legend has it that the stirring *Divertissement à la Hongroise* was inspired by a kitchen maid humming before a fireplace.

Franz would have been perfectly happy at Zelész —at least during these first weeks—if he could only have seen his Viennese friends now and then. In answer to a letter from Schober and some others, in which they reproached him for not writing, he replied:

* Actually it was not the music of Hungary but that of the Hungarian gypsies that so attracted Schubert, and after him Liszt and Brahms. Until recently this gypsy music was accepted generally as native Hungarian, and it is only in comparatively recent years that the Hungarian composers Zoltán Kodály and Béla Bartók discovered what the real music of Hungary is, and recorded and printed it.

Dearest and best friends:

How could I possibly forget you—you who are everything to me! Spaun, Schober, Mayrhofer, Senn, how are
you all? Are you well? I am in the best of health. I live
and compose like a god, as though indeed nothing else in the
world were possible.

Mayrhofer's "Loneliness" is finished, and I think it is
the best thing I have done, for I was carefree when writing
it. I hope you are as well and happy as I am. I am really
alive, thank God! It was high time, for otherwise I should
have merely become just another worthless musician. . . .
Write very soon, all of you: every word from you is precious.

Your ever-faithful friend,
Franz Schubert

The quiet days went by; they were taken up
with lessons for the little Countesses, music in the
evening, excursions through the countryside, and on
Sundays, attendance at the village church. Franz did
not relish these compulsory services. Like his brother
Ignatz he had little sympathy with "organized" religion, and the priests who served it.

Franz's carefree life at Zelész seemed, to his
brothers at home, a completely happy and desirable
existence. Ignatz wrote to him:

"You happy creature! How I envy your lot!
You are enjoying a delicious, golden time of freedom
and can give wing to your musical genius; you may
throw off your thoughts as you like, and are beloved,
admired, idolized; whereas we, miserable school-ush-

ers, the butt of undisciplined youth, have to endure all kinds of rudeness and humiliations, and are in subjection to a public of blockheads."

Before long, however, Schubert began to find life in the country rather dull and uninteresting. He longed for Vienna and the gay friends whose enthusiasm was so stimulating to his music. Here, in spite of the quiet and leisure with which he was surrounded, he could not seem to work so well. Ferdinand had asked him to write a Requiem Mass, and finally, with much more effort than his compositions usually caused him, this was completed. Franz sent it on to his brother with the following letter:

Dear brother Ferdinand: August 24, 1818

It is half-past eleven at night, and your "Requiem" is finished. It made me sad enough, believe me, for I put my whole soul into the writing of it. . . . Things are not going well with you: I wish I could change with you so as to make you happy for once. You would find relief from every heavy burden. Dear brother, I wish with all my heart it were possible. My foot has gone to sleep, and that is very annoying. If the silly thing could write, it wouldn't fall asleep. . . . Good morning, little brother! I fell asleep as well as my foot and am now continuing this letter on the 25th at 8 o'clock in the morning. . . .

In spite of everything going well, and my health being good, I am counting the days till the word goes forth: To Vienna! To Vienna! Yes, beloved Vienna, you hold in your narrow compass the dearest and most precious things in my life, and nothing but the blessed sight of them again will put an end to my longing. . . .

I remain, with love to all, your true and faithful

Franz

Early in October came a welcome break in the monotony of daily life on Count Esterházy's estate. Each year at vintage time the people of Zelész held a special festival to celebrate the gathering of the harvest.

For some time beforehand the peasants had been busy building large *Tristen* or stacks of grain in the fields. These were so constructed that the rain and snow would fall away from their smooth surfaces, and the oats and wheat be kept dry and safe within. Pits had been dug and filled with turnips, carrots, cabbages, and potatoes to last through the long winter months, and great baskets or hoppers of grapes were brought in on the backs of the harvesters, ready to pour into the huge vat where they would be trodden into wine. Now the year's heaviest work was ended, and it was fitting that the occasion should be celebrated with merrymaking and rejoicing.

On the morning of the festival, there was first a special service of Holy Mass and Thanksgiving. The village church was decorated with sheaves of

golden grain and bunches of purple grapes, and the
peasants, dressed in picturesque holiday costume, came
in with their arms filled with vegetables and fruits to
be blessed by the priest.

Presently Count Esterházy and his household arrived. The two little Countesses, with shining curls
and stiffly starched, long white dresses, marched solemnly in with their stylish mother. Karola could
hardly resist skipping as she came up the aisle.

"But where is Herr Schubert, *Mühmchen?*" she
whispered as they seated themselves in a carved pew
specially reserved for the Esterházy family.

"Sh-h- . . ." Countess Rosine replied; "he is
conducting the choir."

By craning her neck, Karola could just make out
the black coat-tails and curly head of their music-
tutor as he rose to direct the village singers and the
improvised orchestra of violin, lute, and guitar.

After the services there was a great feast in the
Count's garden, and all the people of Zelész and the
surrounding country were invited. Long tables groan-
ing with roast meats, cakes and fruit, and great kegs
of wine, had been set up in the orchard under trees
already bright with autumn coloring. Winter begins
early in northern Hungary, and this harvest feast
would be the last outdoor celebration for many months
to come.

When they had all eaten as much as they could

hold, the merrymaking began in earnest. Now the grapes were poured into the big wine vat, and gay, barelegged young couples—the girls with skirts tucked high, and boys with trousers rolled up—jumped in and took turns in treading out the fragrant juice, while the rest of the company danced with hilarious enjoyment to the exciting music of the Hungarian gypsies.

All the musicians of the community were gathered there, so one group could start in playing when another grew tired. Before he realized what he was doing Franz, carried away by the general enthusiasm and the stirring rhythm of the music, seized a violin that had been temporarily abandoned by its owner, and began to join in the playing.

All at once he became conscious of a small figure in white at his elbow. Twilight was falling, and lanterns had been lighted among the trees.

"I didn't know you could play the violin, Herr Schubert!" a demure little voice remarked.

Franz blushed self-consciously, but he did not stop playing. "Oh, that is nothing—any good musician should be able to play several instruments."

Karola leaned against a tree. "Cousin Karl says you are a very wonderful musician," she said, looking at him gravely.

"Oh, but, Fräulein—I mean, Countess Karola . . ." Schubert was so embarrassed that for a moment he lost track of the music he was playing. He had never thought of the little Countess before save as a docile child who really seemed to understand what he tried to teach her. But now, in the half-light of early evening, with her serious face and long white dress, he could almost imagine she was a grown young lady. And suddenly he realized that she was very beautiful.

"Herr Schubert—I should like to dance!" Karola said imperiously. "*Mühmchen* says I am too young, but I think if you would help me . . ."

Without a word Franz put down the fiddle and extended his arms; solemnly the two—the chubby musician and the child in her long white dress—circled among the trees to the tune of the wild Hungarian melodies.

When Ferdinand wrote to thank Franz for sending him the Requiem, Schubert replied:

My Requiem pleased you, you wept during the performance of it, and perhaps at just the same passage as I. My dear brother, that is the highest reward possible for this gift of mine: do not let me hear you speak of any other. If I did not get to know the people about me here better each day, I might be just as contented as I was at the beginning. But I see now that with the exception of one or two really good-hearted girls I have nothing in common with any of them. I long for Vienna more and more each day. We shall set out in the middle of November. . . .

The very things that had seemed most attractive to Franz when he first came to Zelész now lost all interest in his eyes. He wrote to Schober:

Here in Zelész I have to be everything at once: composer, editor, audience, and goodness knows what besides. There is not a soul here with a genuine interest in music except, perhaps, now and then, the Countess (if I am not mistaken). So I am all alone with my beloved [his music] and must hide her in my room, in my pianoforte, and in my own heart. Although this is often very depressing, yet on the other hand it inspires me towards greater things. Do not be afraid that I shall stay away any longer than I absolutely must. . . .

Franz could now think of only one thing: "To Vienna—to Vienna! Yes, beloved Vienna. . . ."

CHAPTER XII

"Vienna—Beloved Vienna!"

IN mid-November the Esterházys left their country estate at Zelész and returned to Vienna. Countess Rosine was delighted to get back to the social whirl of city life, and the two little Countesses looked forward to seeing their friends. But Franz was happiest of them all; he had never been away for such a long period—the four months in the country had seemed like a lifetime to him.

After his return to Vienna, Schubert continued to give music-lessons to the Esterházy children and to join the family in occasional evenings of music. One afternoon, as he was finishing Karola's piano lesson, the Count sent for him.

"Tomorrow we are expecting the visit of an elderly relative of mine," he told Franz. "I should like you to be present in the evening if you can arrange this. Our cousin, Count Stefan, has an extraordinary passion for music." The Count broke off and hesitated a moment. "This passion of his has really unsettled the old man's brain," he went on. "In other things he is normal, but when it comes to music—" Again Count Esterházy hesitated, while Schubert waited in respectful silence for him to continue.

"He imagines he is a great composer," the Count explained. "And nothing enrages him so much as to have this fact doubted. He usually brings with him some new 'composition', and he will surely ask you to play it for him."

"That should not be difficult," said Franz, who was well used to deciphering strange manuscripts.

"But unfortunately Count Stefan does not write real music—anything, that is, that could be actually played. But if, perhaps, you could *pretend* to decipher his manuscript, improvise as you go along . . ."

Schubert hesitated. "That would hardly be honest, sir," he answered gravely.

Count Esterházy laughed. "Do not let that bother you," he replied. "My cousin would not know the difference, and it would be a real service to humor the old gentleman."

Just as Count Esterházy had predicted, his cousin

produced a roll of music when he was introduced to
Schubert.

"What luck!" the old Count cried. "I have a
new work here—just a trifle," he coughed self-consciously, "but rather good, I think. You might like
to try it over."

When Franz opened the manuscript he could
hardly suppress his laughter—a chaos of notes covered
the pages, and all manner of strange black marks.
But without saying a word, he bowed to the old Count
and to the rest of the company, sat down and began to
play. He watched the score carefully, as if he were
actually reading the music before him, and turned the
pages as he went along.

Count Stefan listened with an expression of intense satisfaction, and when Schubert ended with a
brilliant finale, he rose to his feet applauding. "Bravo
—bravo! That was well done, my friend. Not bad,
eh?" he continued, turning to the others.

They all assured him that he had written a masterpiece, but Schubert felt guilty to have tricked the
old man in such a fashion. "I shall have to confess
to him what I have done," he thought to himself.

When Count Stefan begged Schubert the following evening to repeat the performance, Franz hardly
knew what to say. But his patron Esterházy was so
insistent that finally the young composer seated himself once more before the strange manuscript.

First he tried to remember what he had played the day before, but gradually he became so carried away by his own improvising that he went on and on, forgetting to turn the pages of the music.

Count Stefan began to frown and tap the floor with his foot. Finally he rose from his chair and went over to the piano, peering sharply first at the manuscript, and then at the musician.

Schubert came to himself; he began turning the pages once more, and finally brought his playing to a close. The old Count seemed quite satisfied with the applause, but Franz, who had thought of a way to clear his conscience, went over and apologized to Count Stefan.

"Please forgive me, your Excellency," he stammered, "I am afraid I did not play your music just as it was written. I was so inspired by the beauty of your themes that for a time I lost myself in improvising."

"That is quite all right, my boy," the old man answered. "I accept your apology. As a matter of fact your improvising did not spoil my composition at all. I even believe," he concluded, with truly noble largesse, "that your improvising *added* to its general effect!"

Franz was offered a room in the Esterházy home
when the family returned to Vienna; but he did not
take advantage of the opportunity. Father Schubert
also proposed to shelter his wayward son, provided the
latter were willing to resume his old occupation of
schoolteaching. But nothing in the world would have
persuaded Franz to teach school again. He was surer
than ever that it would be better to starve than to exist
chained to a schoolroom.

Then Mayrhofer suggested that Schubert should
come and live with him. The poet's apartment, as
Franz knew only too well, was cold and dark—neither
attractive nor comfortable. But Schubert had such a
warm admiration for his friend, and the two got
along so well together, that the young composer
finally gathered together his few personal belongings
and many manuscripts, and moved into Mayrhofer's
dingy rooms.

It really mattered little to Schubert what his
surroundings were. Only two things counted in his
life: music and friends, and both of these were satisfied in his association with Mayrhofer. The latter
stimulated him to write music, and in return Franz
brought a fresh interest and enthusiasm into the poet's
melancholy existence.

Some years after Schubert's death, Mayrhofer
came to a tragic end. He tried to end his life by
jumping into the Danube, but at that time was rescued

by well-meaning friends. Later he committed suicide by jumping from an upper-story window.

While Schubert lived with the unhappy poet, he would rise every morning at six o'clock, as was always his custom, put on an old, threadbare dressing-gown and begin to write at once. He soon became so absorbed in his work that he would hardly realize that he was only half-dressed, and that the room was dark and cold. Often he would even forget to eat his meager breakfast. He continued working in this way until one o'clock or later. If anyone came in he would call out, without even looking up from his work: "*Grüss Gott!* How are you? Good . . ." and go on with his work.

Josef Hüttenbrenner came frequently to see Franz. He had now taken lodgings in the same building where Mayrhofer had his apartment, and nearly every morning he dropped in to see how Franz was progressing.

While Schubert and Mayrhofer were living together in the Wipplingerstrasse [Hüttenbrenner wrote later in his memoirs], the former every day at 6 o'clock in the morning seated himself at his writing-desk and composed without a break till 1 o'clock in the afternoon, smoking a few small pipes. If I came to see him in the morning, he would play to me what he had ready and wanted to hear my opinion. If I praised a song he would say: "Yes, that was a good poem, and when one has something good the music comes easily, melodies just stream into one, so that it is a real joy. With a bad poem everything sticks; one may make a martyrdom of it, and nothing but dry stuff comes forth. I have often rejected dozens of poems that have been pressed on me."

In the afternoon Schubert usually took a walk around the city, or out into the country, and in the evening he and Mayrhofer would go to some inn— perhaps the *Blumenstöckl* or *Ungarischen Kronen* (Hungarian Crown). Here the "Schubertians" regularly gathered, to sit for hours over a glass of beer or cup of coffee, laughing and singing far into the night.

Spaun and Schober, Senn and Josef Hüttenbrenner and a number of others now formed the celebrated circle. Alfred Stadler had moved to Steyr, and Anselm Hüttenbrenner was temporarily in Graz. Franz, who was especially fond of Anselm, wrote to remonstrate with him for deserting his friends in Vienna:

"What on earth keeps you bound hand and foot in that cursed Graz? Have you fallen under some spell that holds you captive in its terrible ban and makes you forget the rest of the world?"

A little later Schubert discovered what the "spell" was. Then he wrote again:

"A rogue—that's what you are!!! Ten years will probably slip past before you see Vienna again.

First one girl and then another turns his head. Oh, may the Devil take the lot, if you let them bewitch you so! For God's sake get married, and then there will be an end of it. . . ."

During the evenings at the tavern Schubert would sit quietly in a corner, saying little, but ready to applaud every joke and witty remark the others made. He was never much of a conversationalist, but the force of his personality always managed to make itself felt, and the warm response in his kindly eyes, the sincere goodwill that was evident to all, brought a large group of devoted friends around him. There were many different types of personalities in this group, but all were held together by one common bond: a deep love for music. And Franz Schubert was their High Priest.

The fall of 1818 was a period of gaiety and high living for the "Schubertians". Franz was in fine health and spirits after his four months of country life. Once his daily work was finished (he never allowed anything to interfere with that), he was ready for any fun. There would be mock duels with Mayrhofer, sham battles and hilarious singing parties on the streets (to shock the passers-by), and even wild sessions of doorbell-ringing late at night. There was no end to the pranks these young men thought of.

The "Schubertians" were constantly gathering new members. Whenever a strange face appeared,

Franz would ask: *"Kann er was?"* ("What can he do?"), and soon *"Kanevas"* became a popular nickname for the stocky little musician.

Mayrhofer called him *"Schwammerl"*, an Austrian word corresponding to "Fatty". Franz took it all in good fun. He was so lacking in personal vanity, so genuinely devoted to his friends, that he would have been content with any name that it might have pleased them to call him, no matter how derogatory.

Holzapfel once said: "He was a very little man, but he was a giant!"

Although Schubert wrote music in almost every form, including symphonies, quartets, and trios, cantatas, operas, dances and piano pieces, his songs were most successful of all. Everyone who heard them was impressed—but still the publishers refused to put them into print.

Salieri had warned his pupil not to set Goethe's poems to music. Schubert, however, was irresistibly drawn to the famous German's writings, and he gave some of the poems not one, but several different interpretations.

"It is high time Goethe should hear these,"

Spaun had said to him one day a few years before, as he was looking over some of Franz's songs. "If he only knew what beautiful settings you have given his poems I am sure he would recommend you to his friends and publishers."

"I would never dare importune his Excellency!" Franz replied. "Goethe would hardly be interested in my humble interpretations of his immortal lines."

"You are too modest, my Franzl!" Spaun replied. "Does not Vogl himself tell you so? Now if you will make some fresh, neat copies of your songs, I myself will send them with a dedication."

The "fresh, neat copies" proved quite a labor, for Schubert to his surprise found that he had already set more than two score of Goethe's poems to music. When the copies were finally completed, Spaun added the following dedication:

Your Excellency:

The undersigned ventures by means of these lines to deprive you of your precious time for a few minutes in the hope that the enclosed collection of songs may prove a not quite unwelcome gift to your Excellency, and that you will therefore excuse the great liberty he is taking.

The songs collected in this copybook are by a composer named Franz Schubert. He is nineteen years of age. Nature has from his earliest childhood endowed him with the most decided gifts for music, and these have been trained by the Nestor of composers, Salieri, out of a disinterested love of art. The universal applause which the young artist's songs (those which I send herewith and others of his numerous compositions) have gained among connoisseurs and non-connoisseurs of both sexes has encouraged his friends in the wish that the modest youth should begin in earnest his musical career through the publication of a portion of his compositions, whereby there is no doubt that in a short time he will rise to the high position his talent merits. It is proposed to begin with a selection of German songs, which are to be followed by more important instrumental compositions. . . .

The artist cherishes the wish to dedicate these in all humility to your Excellency, to whose glorious poems he attributes not only the inspiration of the greater part of them, but also his own success as a German singer.

Being too modest himself to deem his work worthy of the great honor of bearing on its cover the highly esteemed name known throughout the world wherever the German language is spoken, he has not the courage to ask himself this great favor; and so I, one of his friends, saturated with his melodies, dare in his name to beg it of your Excellency. A special edition worthy of this honor will be prepared. I forbear from any further eulogy of these songs, as they will speak for themselves. I would only add that those which are to follow in no wise fall short of these with regard to melody—in fact, perhaps surpass them in appropriateness and expression, as the pianist who plays the songs to your Excellency will demonstrate.

Should the young artist be fortunate enough to win the approval of him whom more than any other in the wide world he honors, I would venture the request that the permission sought may, in a few words, be graciously communicated.

I remain in all reverence,

Your obedient servant,

JOSEF EDLER VON SPAUN

(dweller in the Landskrongasse, No. 622, 2d floor)

Goethe, however, received only too many such requests from unknown and struggling young composers, who hoped that the illustrious name of Germany's greatest poet would bring recognition to their own work. And so he did not trouble to acknowledge either the gift or the petition for dedication.

Music meant very little to him, really. "I can form no judgment of music," Goethe once wrote, "for I have no knowledge of the means which music employs for its own ends; I can only speak of the impression which music makes on me when I yield myself to its influence."

Goethe lived to be a very old man, and years later, after Schubert himself had passed away, Mme Schröder-Devrient (a celebrated opera singer of her time) sang the "Erlkönig" for the aged poet. It sounded vaguely familiar to him, and he was greatly impressed with her dramatic interpretation.

When she had finished, Goethe, "laying both his hands on the singer's head, kissed her forehead, and exclaimed: 'Thanks, a thousand times, for this grand artistic performance', and went on to say: 'I once heard this composition in my earlier life, and it did not agree with my views of the subject, but, executed as you execute it, the whole becomes a complete picture.' "

Schubert now became convinced that opera was the only medium that would bring him in any money. Had not Salieri always insisted he must devote his talents to writing for the stage?

"You know," he told his friends, "I have always felt that I was destined to write great opera."

Poor Schubert! Until the end of his days this belief possessed him. He wrote opera after opera, and each time faced another defeat. Yet in spite of every failure he continued with undiminished ardor, always hoping that the next effort would bring success.

One day in 1819, Vogl came in while Schubert was working. "Franz," he said, "at last I have found an opportunity to interest the manager of the *Hofoper* [Court Opera] in your music."

Schubert's eyes shone behind his steel spectacles. "Did he really seem interested?" he asked eagerly.

"I think he was," the singer said, looking through a pile of freshly written manuscript. "Have you any new songs for me, Franz?"

"Yes, yes, of course, several," Schubert cried. "But the opera manager—what did he say? Did he think I might write an opera for him?"

Vogl smiled indulgently at his young friend. "He even went so far as to say he would seriously consider producing an opera of yours."

"Not really! Oh, my friend, what luck! What good fortune!"

"I told him that you had a number of scores—"

"Oh, but those would never do!" Franz exclaimed. "Old stuff. No—I must write something new. It is so easy for me to write, you know!" He beamed on Vogl. "When I am really interested, the music flows so quickly—like water."

"As a matter of fact," Vogl continued, "the Herr Direktor suggested a libretto to me. I have it here. . . ." He untied a package he had brought with him. "A work by Hofmann called *Die Zwillingsbrüder* [The Twins]. I don't think much of it, to tell you the truth, but it might be interesting. I could sing the dual role of both twins—they never appear together—and perhaps your music would liven the story up."

Franz pounced on the manuscript with a cry, and began eagerly to turn the pages.

"Here there must be a dance—and this will make a splendid aria for you. Only look at this, Vogl . . ." He began to hum under his breath.

Vogl took up his hat. "I see the opera is practically written already," he said with a laugh.

Schubert, deep in the score, was hardly conscious when his friend departed. He sat down at his desk and began at once to write. In a very short time the opera was completed.

CHAPTER XIII

A Trip to Upper Austria

VOGL and Schubert became close friends during the writing of the new opera. The work was completed in a few weeks, but summer came and the *Hofoper* had not yet found time to produce it.

When the heat began to make life in Vienna a misery, Vogl asked Franz if he would like to accompany him on a trip to Upper Austria. "You have no idea how beautiful the country is there," he told Schubert.

Franz was delighted at the prospect. "I have always wanted to visit the northern part of our country," he said, "to see real mountains and wild, natural scenery. Is it a long journey?"

"Not too long. We will travel in a leisurely way," Vogl answered, "stopping wherever we wish to enjoy the countryside. We must spend some time in Steyr. I was born there, you know, and I have many friends and relatives who will be glad to entertain us."

"And Stadler is living now in Steyr!" Franz cried, more than ever anxious to start on the famous journey.

The next few weeks proved some of the happiest in all of Schubert's short life. Although Vogl was thirty years older than his young friend, the two got along perfectly together. The opera singer was a pleasant and stimulating companion, and Franz felt privileged in having this intimate association with a man of such high character. Wherever they went, Vogl—tall, stately, and rather pompous—led the way, and Schubert's small, rotund figure followed up the rear. (Schober drew an amusing cartoon of the two friends, exaggerating the difference in their sizes.)

They spent the night wherever they found themselves, and if there happened to be a piano, the two would make music together—Vogl singing and Franz accompanying him. Soon there would be an

audience.   No matter how humble the inn or village, an appreciative crowd was sure to gather.

One day the friends came to a quaint little village built on the slope of a mountain.   As they toiled up the winding, cobbled street, they saw high above, through a frame of leafy elm trees, a rambling, ancient monastery flanked with Baroque towers.

"Let us go and visit the monks," Vogl suggested. "I have an idea that our music will earn us a dinner."

It was a long climb, but their efforts were well rewarded.   The monastery commanded a magnificent view over the plains, forests, and blue lakes of the picturesque country.   Within, the long, high-ceilinged refectory was cool and restful, and the monks were overjoyed when the travelers offered to play and sing for them.   Never had they, nor in all the hundreds of years of its existence had the old monastery, heard such music!

Finally the friends reached Steyr, where Vogl had spent his early years, and here they were welcomed on every side.   Franz was delighted to meet his old friend of Konvikt days—Albert Stadler.   While Vogl went to stay with a cousin named Paumgartner, Schubert was quartered with a relative of Stadler's— Herr Schellman, an excellent pianist who was chiefly distinguished because he had five pretty daughters. In the same house lived a Government official with three more daughters.   Then there were Stadler's sister Kathi, and her friend Fritzi. . . . Franz had never known so many pretty girls!

Soon after his arrival Schubert met Herr von Koller, a retired merchant whose chief hobby was music. His daughter Josefine was called Pepi, and she played the piano and sang delightfully. Herr von Koller frequently invited the two Viennese musicians to his home.

"In the house where I am lodging [Franz wrote to his brother Ferdinand], there are eight girls, nearly all pretty. So you see one is kept busy! Herr von Koller, with whom Vogl and I have our meals every day, has a very pretty daughter who is a good pianist and is learning to sing several of my songs. . . ."

There were many parties given for Vogl and Schubert. Everyone was friendly in Steyr; there was much dancing (Franz preferred to watch), laughter, merriment, pretty faces and enthusiastic admiration. Franz for the first time in his life was carefree. What a contrast to his existence in Vienna, where he had to struggle just for daily bread, where publishers scorned his work, and the world passed him by unnoticed!

Here in Steyr he was a person of importance. He not only shone in Vogl's reflected glory, he had a glory all his own. Was not his, Franz Schubert's, the only music these people cared to listen to?—and what

joy to look around at the eager faces that watched him
as he played. Ah, this, Franz felt, was living at last!

Every day there was music at Herr Paumgartner's house, or else at the Kollers'. Fräulein Pepi had
a pleasing soprano voice, and she and Vogl and Schubert often joined in singing together. An idea struck
Franz one evening.

"Let us make a three-part song of the '*Erlkönig*'," he exclaimed.

Vogl's dramatic interpretation of the different
characters in this song was renowned. He smiled in-
quiringly at his young friend. "How do you suggest
we should sing it?" he asked.

Franz ran his fingers through his curly hair.
"You, Vogl, must be the father, of course, and you,
Fräulein Pepi, the child."

"Then *you* will have to be the Erl-King!" cried
Pepi and Vogl with one breath.

Herr Schellman played the accompaniment, and
the three singers competed with each other to see
which could give the best performance. Never was
the stirring legend of the *Erlkönig* sung with such
fervor. Schubert was so pleased that he thought of
writing out a new three-part arrangement of the song.

Herr Paumgartner, Vogl's relative, was also an
ardent music-lover. (When Vogl retired, he went to
live with this gentleman.) He played the 'cello, and

had organized a string quartet. Paumgartner begged
Franz to write some music for this group.

"A quintet, if possible," he suggested, "so that
our friend Schellman can play the piano with us."

Herr Paumgartner's favorite song was Schubert's graceful *"Die Forelle"*. "Couldn't you use
'The Trout' as a theme for this quintet?" he urged.

Schubert was always (or nearly always!) ami-
able in granting requests for compositions. It was no
labor for him to write music, but a pleasure—even a
necessity; and it made little difference what form the
composition took. He set to work on the quintet at
once—his mind so filled with the beauties of his recent trip to Upper Austria, its mountains, lakes, and
waterfalls, that all these found expression in the
rippling, foaming melodies of the work. Its fourth
movement consists of variations on the "Trout" theme,
and it is this movement that gives the Quintet its

name. Scored for violin, viola, 'cello, double bass, and piano, it is one of Schubert's loveliest chamber-music compositions.

August, Franz discovered, was Vogl's birthday month. His friends decided to honor the event with a great celebration, which was to be a surprise to the popular singer of the Vienna *Hofoper*. Stadler offered to write a poem; he withdrew now for a time from the merry group of young people and sat in his room, chewing a pen and covering sheets of paper with endless words. Then he and Franz disappeared together. . . .

Finally the day arrived. Everyone pretended to have forgotten that it was Vogl's birthday. In the evening Schubert and his friend went over as usual to have dinner with the Kollers. Suddenly, from every corner of the house friends rushed out at Vogl with cries of congratulation and good wishes. Herr von Koller served a sumptuous banquet, and following this, of course, there was music.

"We have a new composition to perform this evening," Stadler announced, "written in honor of our beloved Vogl's birthday."

Franz had composed a cantata to Stadler's long poem describing the great singer's various roles and triumphs in such a hilarious way that soon not only was the audience in an uproar, but the three performers (Stadler, Schubert, and Fräulein Pepi) were laughing so that they could scarcely finish their performance.

Before leaving Steyr, Stadler's sister Kathi asked Franz to write in her autograph album. With the solemn expression of a schoolmaster (and a twinkle in his eye), he wrote: *"Enjoy the present so wisely that the past may be pleasant to recollect, and the future not alarming to contemplate!"*

Schubert and Vogl had hoped to visit Salzburg while they were in Upper Austria, but they remained so long in Steyr that there was only time enough left for a brief visit to Linz.

Linz was the home of Franz's oldest friend, Josef Spaun, and the latter, although still in Vienna, had insisted when he heard of the proposed tour that Schubert must stop off at Linz and meet his family there.

So in Linz there were more triumphs for young Schubert, more fervent adulation and admiring audiences. Franz wished he could stay longer, but already it was past mid-September, and Vogl had to get back for rehearsals at the Opera. They returned to Vienna by the river on a "post-boat". A large group of friends came down to see them off.

"Come back soon!" they called as the boat pulled away.

This time Franz was not quite so eager to return

to Vienna as he had been the previous summer, when
he left Zelész with such eager anticipation for his
"beloved Vienna". The "beloved" had not proved
very friendly. . . . Franz thought to himself: "A
prophet is not without honor save in his own country!"

All during the fall and winter of 1819-20,
Schubert waited for his opera *Die Zwillingsbrüder* to
be produced. But the Opera Association kept putting
on other works instead.

"I think they have entirely forgotten *The
Twins*," Franz complained to Vogl. "Why is it
that other composers have such success with their
operas, and I can never even get a hearing? This is
the sixth work I have written for the stage, and not
one has seen the light of day."

"Only have a little more patience, my Franzl,"
Vogl reassured his young friend. "There are always
delays and postponements in these matters. One of
these days—only wait and see! *The Twins* will be
heard, and then there will be a new name to add to
the list of great opera composers."

At last in June came the moment for which
Franz had waited so many years. Posters in front
of the *Hofoper* announced that *Die Zwillingsbrüder*,

by Franz Schubert, would be given the following
week. The "Schubertians" were even more excited
than Franz himself; they planned to attend *en masse*,
with the composer in their midst.

But on the evening of the great event, he was
nowhere to be found. "Our Kanevas is probably
planning to listen from behind the scenes," Schober
remarked to Spaun as they decided they must go on
to the Opera without him.

Actually Schubert was already in the theater,
but not behind the scenes. He was sitting in the gallery with Anselm Hüttenbrenner, who had come in
unexpectedly from Graz that afternoon. Fearful of
a demonstration by his friends, and far too shy to face
the public eye, he had decided to slip in and take his
place in the topmost gallery.

Vogl sang the part of both twins, and did his best
to make the improbable drama convincing. At the
close of the opera there was tremendous applause, but
Franz, leaning down from his gallery seat, felt sure
that most of the clapping came from the section
where his friends were sitting. Others in the audience seemed less enthusiastic—he even imagined he
heard a few hisses. . . .

Then there was a call for the composer. "Schubert—Schubert!"

Franz was really terrified. He sank back in his

seat and tried to hide behind Anselm's broad shoulders.

"They are calling for you, Franz," his friend whispered, nudging him sharply. "You must go down to the stage."

"Oh no, *no*—I couldn't possibly do that!" muttered the bewildered musician.

"Then you must stand up and bow."

Schubert gulped nervously. "I am not dressed . . . You know I do not own a proper evening coat."

"Take mine," Anselm exclaimed, starting to remove his coat and hand it to the trembling composer.

But Franz could not be persuaded to make his presence known. As the cries from the audience continued, Vogl came before the curtain.

"I must thank you in Herr Schubert's name," he said regretfully. "Unfortunately the composer is not present. . . ."

Franz, shaking in his gallery seat, gave a smile of relief to think that he had escaped.

After the performance, the "Schubertians" gathered at the "Flower-pot". (Some of Franz's friends accused him of choosing his taverns because of their picturesque names. The "Black Cat", the "Snail", the "Oak", and the "Flying Horse" were some of his favorites.)

Here they celebrated the success of *The Twins* with several bottles of old *Nessmüller* wine. Franz was supremely happy. His greatest ambition had been achieved.

The critics, however, were not too complimentary about *Die Zwillingsbrüder*.

I would warn this talented young man that too much praise is unwholesome [one of them wrote]. For the public received the operetta as if it were a great masterpiece, which, of course, it was not. Certainly there is evidence in his composition of thoroughness and well-thought-out sequence of new themes, but, just as light frivolous music is not suitable to illustrate heroic subjects, so his music is far too grave and exalted to illustrate this very frivolous subject. Generally speaking I am of the opinion that this young composer (he calls himself Schubert) will employ his talent more happily in the heroic than in the comic line.

Other critics called the music "a pretty trifle. . . . But many of the melodies are somewhat antiquated, and many unmelodious."

In spite of its apparent success, *Die Zwillings-brüder* was performed only six times, and was then dropped from the Vienna Opera repertoire. Schubert would have been terribly disappointed if his interest had not, in the meanwhile, been taken up with

another composition for the stage. The Vienna Theater commissioned him to write incidental music for
a fantasy called *Die Zauberharfe* (The Magic Harp).
Franz completed the score in two weeks' time, and
considered it one of his best works.

But the critics did not like it. They said the
music was "ineffective and fatiguing, the harmonies
too sudden, the instrumentation overloaded. . . ."

Time has proved that Schubert was right, and
not the critics. From *The Magic Harp* has come
some of his most beautiful music, though by error it
is usually called the "Overture to *Rosamunde*".

The Vienna Theater had agreed to pay Schubert
five hundred gulden for his work; but unfortunately
Die Zauberharfe was a failure, and the company went
bankrupt. Franz's dreams of affluence vanished into
thin air. Instead of five hundred gulden, he received
nothing at all.

Money, however, meant very little in Franz
Schubert's life. If he had enough to pay for his food
and lodging, and occasionally to buy a new suit when
his old one was too hopelessly shabby, that was all he
really wanted. Unfortunately there was never enough
for even such small matters. He was always hopelessly in debt.

He continued to write new works for the stage.
Following *The Magic Harp* came an oriental drama

called *Sakuntala*. Again the score interfered with the success of the music.

"Why don't you and Schober do an opera together?" Hüttenbrenner suggested. "It should be much easier to work out an effective result if the libretto and the music are written hand in hand."

Schober enjoyed quite a reputation as a poet among the "Schubertians". He and Franz both became enthusiastic about the idea.

"We will go into the country to work," Schober announced. "I know just the place where we can be as completely quiet and undisturbed as we could wish. The Bishop of St. Pölten is a relative of my mother's; he adores music and would be delighted to have us stay with him. He lives in the castle of Ochsenburg, surrounded by a magnificent park, in one of the most beautiful parts of Austria."

The two friends went to St. Pölten, and stayed there for several weeks with Bishop Nepomuk. Most of the time they worked on the new opera, called *Alfonso and Estrella*. But there were concerts and parties too.

"In Ochsenburg," Schober wrote to Spaun, "we were very busy seeing the beautiful neighborhood and attending balls and concerts in St. Pölten; nevertheless, we were industrious, especially Schubert, who composed nearly two acts. . . . I only wish you had been there to hear the glorious melodies as they came;

it is too wonderful how rich and ever-fresh thoughts pour from him. . . ."

Schubert was so grateful to the good Bishop for his hospitality that he dedicated a group of songs to him.   And the Bishop replied with a warm testimonial to his talented guest:

You have done me a really remarkable and undeserved honor, dear sir. . . . Accept my heartiest thanks for this mark of your regard and for the kind letter which accompanied the copy of your excellent work. . . . God, from whom all good gifts come, has endowed you with such rare and exalted musical talent that its further employment should form the foundation of your future happiness and lasting good fortune.   With every good wish and assurance of my high esteem, I am,

Your very humble servant,

JOHANN NEPOMUK, *Bishop*

Alfonso and Estrella, in spite of all the efforts of Franz's friends and admirers, was no more fortunate than his previous operas—less, in fact, for the *Hofoper* refused even to produce it.

It was not until 1854, thirty-seven years after Schubert's death, that *Alfonso and Estrella* finally was given a public performance.   Schober was living at that time in Weimar, and when he heard that Liszt was interested in Schubert's music, he took the score of the opera to that other great "Franz".   Liszt became one of Schubert's most enthusiastic admirers, and insisted that *Alfonso and Estrella* was even greater than the operas Gluck wrote.

When Schubert returned to Vienna in the fall of 1821, after his visit to St. Pölten, Schober suggested that he come and live with him again. Franz was glad to accept, for he had had enough of Mayrhofer's gloomy apartment.

Schober had recently returned from a visit to Sweden. He had always been pleasure-loving, but now he was more than ever taken up with constant merrymaking and a search for new sensations.

This was all very well as long as it involved only himself, but he insisted on dragging Schubert with him whenever he could persuade his friend to stop working. Franz was not blessed with Schober's iron constitution. Dissipation was ill-suited to his character, and he paid a sad price for his ventures into the world of too much pleasure. Schubert's health was seriously affected, and eventually this was the cause of his tragic early death.

Nothing, however, was allowed to interfere with his music-writing. Mornings were always devoted to composing—but there was no telling when an inspiration might strike him. Sometimes while he was sitting in the tavern, surrounded by a noisy group of friends, an idea would suddenly come into his head.

"Have you any paper?" he would say, searching for his pencil. "Give me that menu card, that's a good fellow!" And in a few minutes the outlines of a masterpiece would be scribbled on the back of any stray paper that came to hand.

Ferdinand Schubert had been appointed choirmaster at Altlerchenfeld, and when Franz visited him there one day, he asked his brother: "Would you like some new music for your next Sunday's services?" Since neither pencil nor music-paper could be found, Schubert took some brown wrapping-paper and a few stray ends of charcoal, and within half an hour he handed his brother a set of special Antiphons for the Palm Sunday service.

The ease and rapidity with which Schubert wrote music was a constant source of amazement to all who knew him. Any time, anywhere, music would come at his beck and call—and even at unwelcome moments it would overwhelm him with a demand for expression.

In the fall of 1919 Josef Hüttenbrenner lay ill in the hospital in Vienna. Franz visited him there, and while sitting by his friend's bedside, a sudden inspiration seized him. He forgot completely the ailing Hüttenbrenner—who took care not to interrupt the flow of genius.

Schubert began to write. . . . Three hours later he came back to earth and realized that he was still in the hospital, and that his dinner hour had long since passed. On the score of the music—a Piano Overture for four hands—he wrote:

Written in November in Herr Josef Hüttenbrenner's room at the Hospital, within the space of three hours, and dinner missed in consequence.

CHAPTER XIV

"Schubertiades"

ANNA, Josefine, Kathi, and Barbara Fröhlich
were called, by their many friends and admirers, the "Four Graces". They were
all attractive young women, and accomplished musicians as well, and their home was a meeting place for many of the artists, poets, and composers
of Vienna.

Leopold Sonnleithner went often to call on the
four sisters. One day he brought them one of Schubert's songs. As he was playing it through, Fräulein
Kathi looked up in surprise.

"What are you playing there, Herr Sonnleithner?" she asked. "It is beautiful—really quite out
of the ordinary."

Her older sister Anna, teacher of singing at the

Vienna Music Conservatory, went over to the piano and examined the manuscript. She was a small, dark-haired young woman of twenty-three, vivacious, affectionate, and temperamental.

"You are quite right, Kathi," she exclaimed. "This *is* something unusual. Only look, Josefine. . . ."

Josefine Fröhlich had recently made her debut on the concert stage. "What is it, Anna—a new song?"

Only Barbara, youngest of the sisters, continued with her work unmoved. She was sitting at the window painting a bouquet of flowers. They were all talented, the Fröhlich sisters, but Kathi was the most beautiful of the four. Tall and slender, with a lovely oval face and flashing black eyes, her charm and joyous disposition fascinated everyone.

Music was Kathi's greatest passion. "She intoxicates herself with music as others do with wine," the poet Grillparzer said. "When she hears good music she no longer has any control over herself, and is completely carried away."

"I thought you would like this song," Sonnleithner said. "It was written by a friend of mine; I used to go to school with him at the Konvikt. Mark my words, the world will hear from this Franz Schubert."

"And has he written other songs as good as this?"

asked Fräulein Anna after the four sisters had tried
over the manuscript with growing enthusiasm.

Sonnleithner smiled. "Dozens—hundreds, perhaps. Schubert turns out songs as easily as I write
letters."

Kathi Fröhlich clasped her hands. "Why
haven't you told us about this man of genius before?
Bring him to visit us soon—we can't wait to meet
him."

Schubert was received into the Fröhlich family
with warm appreciation. The sisters were fascinated
with his songs, and never tired of singing them while
he accompanied. He had only to look up as he was
playing, to see the "Four Graces" bending over the
piano, listening to his every note with unaffected joy.

Franz, his round face beaming with delight,
loved especially to watch Kathi's black eyes fill with
sympathetic tears, or flash with sudden enthusiasm as
he played—now in melancholy strain, now in stirring
martial rhythm. In those moments he truly expressed
himself. No mere speech could, indeed, so interpret
the deep emotions of the heart as music, which is the
language of the soul.

Unfortunately not everyone could understand
this speech. When Schober once teased Franz because he seemed so indifferent to women, the latter
confessed to him:

"I am not really indifferent, my friend. A

pretty woman is a delight to any man. But alas, I
have no success with the creatures. I can't talk to
them. . . . What they want is to be told that they
are beautiful and desirable. When I search my mind
for pretty speeches, music is all that I can find!"

Schubert may not have fallen in love with the
Fröhlich sisters, but at least they understood his
language and proved themselves warm and sympathetic friends. Kathi wrote of him:

His was a magnificent soul. He was never jealous or
grudging to others, as is the case with so many people. On
the contrary, he was overjoyed when beautiful music was
performed. He folded his hands and placed them against
his mouth, and sat there as if in ecstasy. The purity of his
mind, the lack of all thought of guile, are beyond expression.
Often he would sit down with us on the sofa and rub his
hands and say: "Today I have composed something with
which I believe I have been really successful."

Shortly after Schubert's introduction to the four
sisters, another "immortal" was brought to the Fröhlich household. Grillparzer, tall, with blue eyes and
light hair, and destined to become the greatest Austrian poet and dramatist of his day, had already made
a name for himself.

The first time he visited the Fröhlichs he hardly
noticed Fräulein Kathi. But when he came the second time, Schubert was playing, and Kathi was watch-

ing him with such intense absorption that she hardly noticed the poet's arrival.

Grillparzer's attention became focussed on the eager young girl. He was struck by her beauty and the deep sensitivity with which she listened to the music. He felt as if he had been given an unexpected glimpse into a rare and beautiful soul. When Franz finished playing he went over, and without speaking took both her hands in his and looked long and deeply into her eyes. The following day he brought her a poem entitled: "Silent she sat there, the loveliest of them all."

This was the beginning of a deathless romance. Grillparzer loved the fair Kathi all the rest of his life. Their attachment never blossomed into marriage, but he called her his "eternal affianced", and wrote countless poems to tell her of his love. Many of these poems Schubert set to music.

Leopold Sonnleithner's father was a distinguished patron of music. He had known intimately all the great artists of his day; Haydn, Mozart, Beethoven, and Salieri had all been his personal friends. Herr Sonnleithner was a man of considerable wealth, and each Friday he invited a hundred or more guests to come to his home and listen to music. Sometimes he himself sang—he had a fine bass voice, and the leading musicians of Vienna were heard in his drawing-room.

Schubert's *Prometheus* (written originally for Professor Watteroth) had been performed two years before at the Sonnleithner home. Now Leopold wanted his father to give some of Franz's songs a hearing.

Anna Fröhlich added her plea. "Please do include the '*Erlkönig*'," she begged; "it is the most dramatic of all Schubert's songs."

There was an unusually large gathering of Vienna's fashionable society on the evening the "*Erlkönig*" was performed. Franz kept very much in the background, but he was delighted to find an old friend there whom he had not seen for some time—Count Esterházy's young cousin, the Baron Schönstein.

"What good fortune that we are to hear the '*Erlkönig*' this evening," Karl Schönstein told Franz. "You remember how enthusiastic I was about it in Zelész!"

The song had a tremendous success. Everyone wanted to know about the composer. "Who is this Franz Schubert?" they asked. "And who is his publisher?"

When Herr Sonnleithner asked this last question of Schubert himself, the young musician blushed and looked very much embarrassed. "No one seems willing to take a chance on an unknown composer, sir," he answered, trying to make a joke out of a sensitive subject.

"But this 'Erlkönig' now," the elder Sonnleithner insisted, "it couldn't help selling! Why don't you publish it yourself?—you would soon get your money back."

Franz felt still more embarrassed, but he was too honest to make any false pretenses. "I have no money, sir! And if I had—" he went on ruefully, "it would all go to my tailor—and my shoemaker—and the landlord—and the tavern-keepers. . . ." His voice trailed off into silence.

Herr Sonnleithner cleared his throat gruffly. "So-o-o," he said with a sympathetic glance at the young musician. "Well, something should be done about it."

And something *was* done. Grillparzer, the Baron Schönstein, Herr Sonnleithner, and another friend put their heads together and decided that they would together finance the publishing of the "Erlkönig". Diabelli, the Viennese music-publisher who had been too prudent to take the risk alone, was quite willing to accept a paid commission to print the music.

At the next concert Herr Sonnleithner arrived with a hundred freshly printed copies of the new song. On the cover, in large letters stood:

Der Erlkönig
By Franz Schubert   Opus 1

"This evening," Herr Sonnleithner told the audience, "Franz Schubert's '*Erlkönig*' will be repeated by special request.   And if anyone is interested in subscribing for a copy—" he held up the pile of music—"it can now be obtained in printed form." At the end of the evening every copy had been sold.

The four benefactors decided they would take the proceeds of the sale and print another of Schubert's songs.   This time it was "Gretchen at the Spinning-Wheel", which was marked "Opus 2".   And following this came a collection of several songs, bound together in one volume—then another group, and another.   Each collection was more successful than the last.

Wherever Schubert's songs were heard, his popularity increased.   But so far these had only been performed in private circles.   Now came an opportunity for a wider audience.   Herr Sonnleithner organized a large charity concert at the Kärntnerthor Theater and asked Vogl to sing the "*Erlkönig*".   "And you must accompany him," he told Franz.

Schubert, however, could not bear the thought of facing a large audience.   "That is kind of you, Herr Sonnleithner," he stammered, "but really—I don't believe—" He took a deep breath.   "If you *could* find someone else, I think it would be better!"

Anselm Hüttenbrenner came to Vienna on a visit from Graz (he was now permanently established there) just at that time, and took Schubert's place at the piano. He finally persuaded the bashful young composer to sit beside him on the platform—well away from the audience!—and turn the pages.

As usual, the *"Erlkönig"* took the people by storm. All during Schubert's lifetime he was to be famous chiefly as a writer of songs. It has only been since then that he has come to be appreciated for his many other compositions, equally beautiful—the inspiring symphonies, and the wealth of chamber music and piano works.

It was the custom of the period for musicians to dedicate their works to influential people, who in return for this compliment would send the composer a handsome gift. It had never occurred to Franz to try this with his music, but now, on the suggestion of Schober and Vogl, he inscribed a number of his newly printed songs to some of Vienna's wealthy music patrons.

The result was all that Schubert had hoped for. He wrote to Spaun: "I must tell you that my dedications have not missed their mark: namely, the Patriarch [Ladislaus Pyrker] has been good for 12 ducats, and Friess on Vogl's intervention for 20, which is splendid for me."

Schubert's lucky star seemed really to have risen at last. He might have been in comfortable circumstances for the rest of his life if only he had been fortunate enough to find a trustworthy music-publisher, or if he himself had had a better instinct for business. In this latter respect he differed greatly from—say—Beethoven or Brahms, both of whom had the business instinct, knew where to sell their compositions, and insisted on getting paid fairly.

Diabelli, however, was anything but honest in his dealings with the guileless young Schubert. Seeing what success the privately printed songs were having, he offered to take over the publishing himself, and managed the accounts in such a way that there was little left over for the unfortunate composer. A little later Diabelli suggested that he would buy the earlier songs outright. He offered Franz 800 thalers (about $350); this seemed a fortune to the poverty-stricken Schubert, and he accepted the offer gladly.

During the next few years, however, Diabelli profited enormously by his purchase. From one song alone ("The Wanderer") he made close to $3500 profit, while Franz, all unsuspecting, continued in his bitter poverty.

All through his life Schubert was to suffer from his publishers. He was so mild and undemanding that they took advantage of him at every turn. They even cut out passages of his works that did not please them, and changed some of the titles. Schubert once came across a composition entitled *Trauerwalz*. "What donkey could write a 'sad' waltz!" he exclaimed. Then he discovered that it was one of his own compositions rechristened without his knowledge by the publishers!

But at least for the time being Schubert was out of debt. He had no understanding of the value of money. Whenever a royalty payment came in, he would first pay back the money he owed, and then there would be a celebration for the "Schubertians". After all, thought Franz, what could be better than to share with friends! For was it not they who had inspired his music in the first place?

This was a happy period in Schubert's life. Mornings were given to composing, afternoons usually found him at the Fröhlichs', and evenings were spent either at the tavern, with a group of jolly friends, or at some party where his own music was the center of attraction.

"Schubertiades" Kathi named these functions, and they soon became the most popular form of entertainment among the young people of the Fröhlichs' acquaintance. They would gather at one house or another, play games, recite poetry (Grillparzer often took his latest poems to read), dance, and always end up with the most important part of all—Schubert's music and the singing of his songs. During this period he was writing many dances especially for his young friends and the "Schubertiades".

Sometimes they went on excursions into the country. One Sunday morning early in July, it was decided to drive to Atzenbrugg, a few miles outside of Vienna, and picnic on the meadows in front of the castle there.

At ten o'clock Schubert heard the sound of wheels on the cobblestones below his window; looking down he saw a rented chaise full of laughing young "Schubertians" just driving up. Kathi, Anna, and Josefine Fröhlich sat in the back seat. Facing them were Barbara, a friend of hers, and Luise Gosmar, singing pupil of Fräulein Anna's. Vogl was driving the two horses, and with him were sitting Grillparzer and Leopold Sonnleithner. A young painter named Leopold Kupelwieser stood holding to the side of the carriage, while Schober waved to Franz from the ledge behind. Large hampers of food could be seen beneath the seats.

"Hurry, Franz!" they called. "We still must pick up Hüttenbrenner and Senn."

Schubert gasped. "Are we *all* going in one

carriage?" he asked. "Surely there is not enough
room. . . ."

The young people laughed as if this were some
tremendous joke. "Lots of room, my Schwammerl,"
Schober cried; "I have saved a place for you here beside me."

"Glorious day, *nicht wahr, Herr Schubert?*"
Fräulein Kathi remarked, screwing her head around
so she could look up at Franz as he climbed to the
ledge behind her. The girls were all in light-colored
dresses, high-waisted in the prevailing Empire fashion. They wore large-brimmed hats and gaily
trimmed poke-bonnets, and Franz thought the carriage looked like a garden full of flowers surrounded
by big black beetles. (The beetles were himself and
his companions in their black coats and top-hats!)

It was a gay party; they went laughing and
singing along their way. The fields were spangled
with daisies, buttercups, and bright red poppies, the
birds were singing, and Franz's head was so full of
music—or was it his heart?—that he felt he could
hardly stand so much beauty and happiness.

They had been driving about half an hour when
suddenly the chaise gave such a violent lurch that the
passengers were nearly thrown into the ditch.

"*Donnerwetter*, what has happened?" cried
Vogl, pulling in the horses. With screams of pretended terror the young ladies were helped down

from the carriage. Everything was excitement and confusion. Finally it was discovered that one of the shafts had broken in two. The young people were indignant to think they had been given such a ramshackle vehicle; the men swore under their breaths as they tried to repair the damage, while the girls did their best to soothe them.

Franz walked up and down, looking very ferocious. "I must not get angry," he muttered to himself. "For God's sake I must not get angry. For if I do—" he looked with mock fury at Fräulein Gosmar, "if I do lose my temper I knock all the teeth out of the mouth of the wretch who has angered me!"

The young Fräulein looked at him in frightened surprise. "Do you get angry very often, Herr Schubert?" she asked.

Schubert burst out laughing. "Never—yet!" he answered.

"That is true," Schober replied. "No one has ever seen our Schwammerl in a temper. He puts us all to shame. . . ."

Good-humor was now restored to everyone, and, the chaise having been repaired, the party reached Atzenbrugg without any further complications.

It was a day to remember! The "Schubertians" rollicked and played games like a crowd of merry children. Kupelwieser made a watercolor sketch of

the party, while Franz entertained them with his guitar. Then, seated under a chestnut tree they unpacked the hampers and fell on the contents with ravenous appetites. The young ladies had all contributed something to the feast, each of them anxious to prove her excellence as a cook, while the men had brought wine, fruit, and the Viennese specialty, *Marzipan* (almond-paste candy), molded into miniature pigs, pipes and vegetables.

After lunch they stretched out on the grass while Grillparzer read a number of his poems aloud, and Vogl sang. Then, with Franz accompanying on his guitar, they began to sing *"Heidenröslein"*, *"Gretchen am Spinnrade"*, *"Der Wanderer"*, and many more of Schubert's songs that were old and dear, and also a new one from a manuscript he had brought in his pocket.

Twilight was falling as they drove back to Vienna, and still the young friends sang—quiet, happy songs that filled them with a soft and melancholy contentment. "How good life really is," thought Franz to himself, "and how simple it would be if men could only forget their strife and struggles and live in peace and contentment."

Leopold Sonnleithner had recently become engaged to Anna Fröhlich's singing pupil, Luise Gosmar. Luise was a great favorite with the four sisters, and when her birthday arrived they wanted to plan something special by way of celebration.

"We have no money to buy her a present," Kathi told Grillparzer, "so you will have to write a poem in honor of the occasion."

The poet could never refuse Fräulein Kathi's requests. "Perhaps I will," he answered, "if something occurs to me!"

A few days later he brought her a poem entitled *"Leise flehen meine Lieder"* ("Softly come my songs imploring").

At once Kathi took this to Schubert. "And now you must compose a musical setting!" she begged. "Something that Josefine can sing, with chorus accompaniment. We shall surprise Luise by serenading her beneath her window."

Franz took the poem and read it through. "Beautiful!" he exclaimed. "This is really beautiful." He stared for a moment at the written words; then he lifted his head and smiled. "I have it! It's done already. But let us call it *'Ständchen'*, since it is meant as a serenade for Fräulein Gosmar."

In three days Schubert brought the finished copy of what was to become one of his most beloved songs: "Serenade". The sisters were delighted, but when they discovered that he had written a chorus for men's voices instead of women's they asked him to change it.

"We can't use this," Josefine explained. "You see, Anna's pupils from the Conservatory are to sing the chorus."

"That's easy," Franz replied, rapidly transposing the chorus into a higher key.

The proposed serenade was kept a deep secret. While Fräulein Gosmar was in another part of the house, they moved the piano into the garden, and the singers hid themselves among the trees. When Luise returned to her room, she was suddenly greeted by the sound of lovely singing beneath her window.

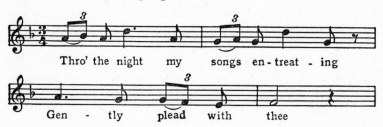

Thro' the night my songs en-treat - ing

Gen - tly plead with thee

When the serenade was ended, Kathi Fröhlich looked for Schubert to see if their performance of his song had pleased him. But the composer was nowhere to be found; he had gone to the tavern that afternoon and had forgotten completely about the whole affair.

Schubert was very forgetful. When he became engrossed in something, the rest of the world went out of his mind. And yet his friends could not hold it against him—he was so penitent when he discovered what he had done. Even Vogl, who could not bear to be kept waiting five minutes, would forgive his young friend any inconvenience. He once remarked: "We must all bend before Schubert's genius, and if he does not come we must creep after him on our knees."

Everyone admired Fräulein Gosmar's "Serenade" so much that it was decided to give a public performance of it at a special concert of the Musik-verein. This time Schubert was reminded more than once to be present.

But again he forgot! Fräulein Anna was in great distress. "This is really too bad!" she exclaimed. "Doesn't anyone know where that naughty Schwammerl is hiding himself?"

A friend offered to look in a near-by tavern. As luck would have it, there was Franz, about to enjoy a second glass of beer. He hurried over to the concert, and was just in time to hear his "Serenade".

"Really," he said later to Fräulein Anna, "I had no idea it was so beautiful!"

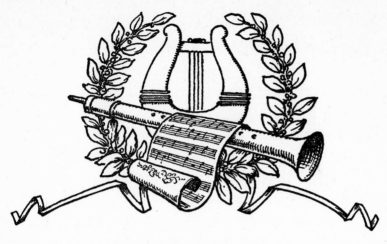

CHAPTER XV

"My Dream"

"SCHOBER — Hüttenbrenner . . . look!"
Schubert exclaimed. He was sitting with
his companions in a corner of the "Flower-
pot" tavern. Do you see who is just coming
in? God be praised, it is Herr van Beethoven himself!"

Schober pulled Franz back into his seat. "What
is so unusual about that? Surely this is not the first
time you have seen Beethoven. After all, you have
both lived in the same city for a good many years."

"But he so seldom goes out any more," Schubert
answered, still red with excitement. "In these last
years, since he has become completely deaf, he no
longer wants to talk with anyone."

"Is it really possible," said Hüttenbrenner, "that

237

you two have never met?" He looked over to the other side of the room, where the celebrated composer and a companion were just seating themselves. "That is Schindler with him. I know Herr Schindler well if you desire an introduction. . . ."

"No—no," answered Schubert nervously. "I would not presume."

Schober leaned forward. "Franz, I don't understand you. Here you have worshiped Beethoven all your life, and yet you have never even tried to make his acquaintance."

"He moves in very exalted society," Schubert murmured. "He has probably never even heard my name. . . ."

"Nonsense!" Schober fairly snorted in his indignation. "Your music is just as fine as his—"

"Please, *please!*" Franz was genuinely distressed.

"But it *is*," Schober insisted. "Perhaps Beethoven doesn't know your work—it's true that for some time he has been unable to attend concerts. Why don't you dedicate one of your compositions to him, and deliver it yourself?"

Franz was abashed at the suggestion; but later, as he thought the matter over, he decided it was not such a bad idea after all. He had recently composed a *Fantasia* for piano, four hands, which rather pleased him.

A few days later Beethoven's slatternly servant

answered a knock at her master's apartment to find a small, self-conscious little man standing at the door.

"I— I have— Is your master at home?" he stammered.

The servant looked him over with some contempt. Certainly this was not one of Herr van Beethoven's high-born friends. This visitor looked very shabby and unpretentious. Perhaps he was a bill-collector.

"I will see," she answered shortly. "What is the name?"

"Schubert," said the little man, twisting his hat nervously, "Franz Schubert."

She did not ask him to come in, but left him standing on the stair-landing. As he waited Franz grew more and more nervous; he was amazed at his own audacity in trying to gain an audience with the idol of his dreams.

When the servant returned he did not even wait for her to speak.

"Give this to Herr van Beethoven, please," he said, thrusting a manuscript into her hands. And before the astonished woman could collect her wits, he crammed his hat on the back of his head and hurried away down the stairs.

Schubert had not seen much of his family since leaving the shelter of his father's home. Ignatz and Ferdinand were now married, and Karl had begun to make a name for himself as a landscape painter. (In the last year of his life, Schubert recommended Karl for a drawing-master's position in Graz. "He is highly skilled, both as a landscape painter and also as a draughtsman," he wrote. "If you could manage to do something for him in this affair, I should be infinitely grateful. . . . My brother is married and has three children, and he would therefore be very glad to find himself in an assured position.")

Father Schubert, with his second wife and their four children (there were nineteen children in all, counting the fourteen of the first marriage!), had now moved from the school in the Lichtenthal district to another in Rossauer. Since Franz had refused to return to his position as schoolteacher, there had been a certain estrangement between himself and his father. This had always weighed on Franz's sensitive heart, and he brooded over it so much that he often dreamed terrifying nightmares, in which his father pursued him relentlessly.

One day in the summer of 1822 Franz had an unusually vivid dream, which made such a deep impression on him (part of it seemed so strangely to portray his own life) that he set down an account of it in his diary:

"My Dream"

July 3, 1822

I was one of many brothers and sisters. We had a good father and mother. I felt a deep love for them all. One day my father took us to a feast. My brothers became very merry there. But I was sad. My father then came up to me and bade me taste the delicious foods. But I could not, and at that my father in his anger banished me from his sight. I turned on my heel, and, with a heart filled with infinite love for those who scorned it, I wandered off into a far country. For years I was torn between the greatest love and the greatest sorrow. Then came news of my mother's death. I hastened back to see her, and my father, softened by grief, did not hinder my return. I saw her lying dead. Tears poured from my eyes. I saw her lying there, looking just as she used to, one with the dear past in which, according to her wishes, we ought still to live and move and have our being.

We followed her mourning to the grave, and the coffin slowly sank. From this time onwards I stayed at home again. Then one day my father took me once more into his pleasure-garden. He asked me if it pleased me. But the garden was hateful to me, and I did not dare reply. Then he asked me a second time, and more impatiently, if I liked the garden. Trembling, I told him no. At that my father struck me and I fled. For the second time I turned away, and, my heart filled with infinite love to those who scorned it, I wandered once more into distant lands. Through long, long years I sang my songs. But when I wished to sing of love it turned to sorrow, and when I wanted to sing of sorrow it was transformed for me into love.

So was I divided between love and sorrow.

And once a pious maiden who had just died appeared to me. And a circle formed about her tomb in which many youths and old men wandered as though in perpetual bliss. They spoke softly so as not to wake the maiden.

Heavenly thoughts like bright sparks seemed to flicker unceasingly out of the virgin's tomb, and to fall in a soft-sounding shower on to the young men. I longed to walk there too. But only by a miracle, so people said, could one enter the circle. I went forward, however, slowly and devoutly, with my eyes lowered towards the gravestone, and before I knew it I was in the circle, from which the loveliest melody sounded. And I felt, pressed as it were into a moment's space, the whole measure of eternal bliss. My father I saw, too, loving and reconciled. He folded me in his arms and wept. And I still more.

FRANZ SCHUBERT

For days after he woke from this curious dream, Franz still felt the spell of the vision he had seen. He became convinced that the "pious maiden" represented the spirit of music, and that by entering into the circle which surrounded her, he had been initiated into the inner brotherhood of harmony—harmony not only of sound but of all relationship. Music more beautiful than any he had ever known now haunted his days and nights. But when he tried to capture it on paper it fled into the skies. At last he gave up trying and devoted himself to other works.

Months passed. Schubert always loved the au-

tumn pageant, and one day in late October he went
walking alone in the Wienerwald.   The forest was
aflame with color; as Franz looked about him in wonder and delight, he was suddenly filled with a compelling urge to write music.   The vision of his strange
dream had never entirely left him, and it may well be
that this was the inspiration of the force that now
moved him.

In a mood of unusual elation Franz continued
his walk through the forest, and as he went, the elusive
threads of his vision wove themselves into a pattern
of unearthly beauty.   At last, trembling with emotion,
he reached for his notebook and jotted down some of
the themes.

Then Schubert hurried back to his room and began to write. Faster and faster the notes spilled on

to the paper; he continued writing until finally in exhaustion he fell asleep at his desk.

The following morning he resumed his work at daybreak—on and on, until two movements of a mighty symphony lay finished beneath his hand. But when he read over what he had written, he was not satisfied. How far inferior to the exquisite harmonies he had dreamed!

The inspiration left him as suddenly as it had come. Try as he would, he could not finish the last two movements which would complete the symphony.

Finally Franz laid the manuscript away in a drawer. Unfinished work was contrary to his orderly nature. In his disgust he almost threw the pages into the fire. . . .

Yet, if Franz Schubert had only known, this "Unfinished" Symphony was actually one of the most perfect works of his entire lifetime—a masterpiece so tenderly beautiful, and at the same time so simple, that through the ages it has spoken to all hearts. Truly it contains, in the words of Franz's dream, "heavenly thoughts like bright sparks . . . the whole measure of eternal bliss".

The following year, through the recommendation of Anselm Hüttenbrenner in Graz, the leading musical society of that town sent Schubert an invitation to become a member of their organization.

The services which you have rendered to the art of music are too well known for the Committee of the Styrian Society of Musicians to be in ignorance thereof [wrote the Secretary of the Society]. In their name I am therefore deputed to inform you that as a proof of their recognition and esteem, you are elected an honorary member. . . .

To this Franz replied thanking them for the honor, and added:

May my devotion to the art of music succeed in making me worthy one day of this distinction. In order to express my liveliest thanks in music as well I will make so bold as to present your honored Society at the earliest possible date with the score of one of my Symphonies.

Schubert, however, did not feel in the mood for writing symphonies at that time. Months went by, and Franz, who was usually the soul of honor, had not yet sent the symphony. A year later Herr Schubert asked his son if the promised manuscript had been dispatched. Franz suddenly remembered the symphony in B minor that he had begun and then had laid away in his drawer. He decided to send on what he had written and forward the rest when he should get around to writing it.

But the last two movements were never written. Anselm Hüttenbrenner kept the fragment, waiting to turn it over to the Styrian Music Society when Schubert should send him the remainder. Then he too forgot about the manuscript, and it did not come to light for many years. The first performance of this *Unfinished* Symphony—most universally popular of all Schubert's music—was not to be given until thirty-seven years after the composer's death and forty-two years after he had composed it. That it was eventually heard was due to the enterprise of a Vienna conductor named Herbeck, who—having learned that Hüttenbrenner had had the score all this time—went to him and induced him to allow it to be played. And so it was—at a Friends of Music concert in Vienna on December 17, 1865.

The *Unfinished* was not by any means the only Schubert work to disappear and then turn up many years afterward. An interesting story is told of how some others of his "buried" scores were discovered. In 1867 two young Englishmen—George Grove and Arthur Sullivan (who was later to collaborate with Gilbert in the famous operettas)—made a special pilgrimage to Vienna. It was their idea that somewhere in Vienna there must be a good many Schubert manuscripts, as yet unpublished—their very existence, perhaps, unknown. The two went to the music-publisher Spina, who had succeeded to the Diabelli business, and asked him if he had any Schubert scores put away. Old Spina could not remember, but he led them to a storage room and told them: "Take a look through those piles of manuscript—you may find something."

Through hundreds of dusty sheets they searched, turning everything over in the hope of finding *something* by Schubert.   Presently they were rewarded with a song—then another—then some church music. "Their pile of loot grew higher with every hour.   By midnight they had recovered all the lost part-books of *Rosamunde*, a Trio, a *Stabat Mater*, and a great many songs.   At two in the morning they stopped, played a triumphant game of leap-frog around Spina's room, and called it a day." *

Shortly after Schubert wrote the *Unfinished* Symphony his health began to fail.   He had never been very robust, and his long hours of work, the night life at the taverns, and insufficient food, brought on a state of anemia that made him an easy victim to disease.

Early in 1823 he became seriously ill—an illness from which he never entirely recovered.   At that time he was taken to a hospital, and although he slowly began to improve, he became terribly despondent.   His friends visited him in the hospital, but nothing they could say would make the unfortunate man believe he would ever be well again.

And yet he continued to write music.   The faithful Josef Hüttenbrenner came every day to visit his beloved Schubert.   (Franz almost resented the ador-

* From *An Almanac for Music-Lovers*, by Elizabeth C. Moore. Henry Holt & Co., New York, 1940.

ing esteem with which Anselm's brother regarded him. Once he remarked in a half-affectionate, half-contemptuous way: "That Josef Hüttenbrenner—he thinks *everything* I do is perfect!")

Hüttenbrenner, trying to rouse Franz from his apathy, suggested writing to the famous music-publishing house of Peters in Leipzig, to see if they would be interested in bringing out some of Schubert's compositions.

"Try if you wish," Franz agreed, indifferently; "but I know in advance what their answer will be."

Hüttenbrenner sent a letter to the Leipzig publishers:

"Among the local newer composers in Vienna, there is now a talent which is already attracting attention and has become a favorite with the public here. In short, speaking without exaggeration, he is a second Beethoven—indeed, that immortal man has already said of him, 'This one will surpass me.' " (Was the worthy Hüttenbrenner drawing on his imagination, or had Beethoven indeed been impressed by the composition that Schubert had sent him?)

The reply, however, was just what Franz expected. Messrs. Peters sent good wishes, but said they could not take a chance on a composer who was completely unknown in northern Germany.

Schubert was able to leave the hospital in a few

weeks, but later his illness returned with even greater force, and he was beside himself with misery.

I feel myself to be the most unfortunate and the most wretched man in the whole world [he wrote to the young painter Kupelwieser, who was now studying in Rome]. Picture to yourself someone whose health is permanently injured, and who, in sheer despair, does everything to make it worse instead of better; picture to yourself, I say, someone whose most brilliant hopes have come to nothing, someone to whom love and friendship are at most a source of bitterness, someone whose inspiration (whose creative inspiration, at least) for all that is beautiful threatens to fail, and then ask yourself if that is not a wretched and unhappy being.

But Schubert's "creative inspiration" did not really fail him. Out of his despair he distilled an even greater expression of beauty. He was vaguely conscious of this himself.

"Sorrow sharpens the understanding and strengthens the character," he wrote in his diary; "whereas happiness seldom troubles about the former, and only makes for weakness or frivolity in the latter." And again: "All that I have created is born of my understanding of music and my own sorrow; that which is engendered only by grief seems to please the world least of all."

Just as Schubert was beginning to wonder if he would ever be well and happy again, he received a visit from his former patron, Count Esterházy.

"We are going to Zelész again this year, to re-main there from May until October," the Count said, looking around Schubert's bare and untidy room with a pitying yet contemptuous glance. "My wife and daughters do not like to be without music for so long a time. They thought perhaps you would come with us for the five months. I am prepared," he added, "to pay you five hundred thalers for the period men-tioned."

Schubert bowed low. "That is very kind of you, your Excellency," he said, hesitating a little. "I have not been very well lately; perhaps a stay in the country would be helpful. . . ."

"It should be just the thing for you," Count Esterházy assured him. "Then it is settled? You can come by post-chaise at your convenience."

Schubert was glad to get away from Vienna. He arrived at Zelész late in the evening, and at the village inn (where the post-chaise stopped) was met by the lodge-keeper. The latter took him, not to the room he had had before in the estate-agent's cottage, but to the castle itself. Franz could not help smiling a little. Apparently his growing reputation in Vienna now en-titled him to move a step higher on the social ladder.

The following morning he wakened early, and jumping from his bed threw open the shutters to let the sunshine in. Just below the window, a bush of fragrant lilac greeted him with delicate perfume.

The grass at the edge of the graveled court was covered with tiny marguerites, and under the trees he
could see lilies-of-the-valley half-hidden in their pale
green leaves.

Beyond the courtyard was the orchard, now gay
with apple-blossoms and white-veiled cherry trees.
Franz remembered this same orchard in its autumn
coloring, at the time of the harvest festival on his last
visit to Zelész. He thought of the little Countess
Karola, who had danced with him in her long white
dress. She would be a grown young lady now. . . .

Just at that moment there was a clatter of hoofs,
and a young girl on a large gray horse dashed into the
courtyard below.

"Fritz!" she cried, "come quickly and take
Shadow to the stables."

A groom rushed out and seized the horse's bridle.
As the girl leapt to the ground she happened to glance
up towards Schubert's window. He caught his breath
at the radiant vision of her face, heart-shaped and
flushed from the wind, with large, expressive dark
eyes, and black hair blown into a tangle of curls.
Then suddenly he was conscious of his informal attire.

"Good-morning, Herr Schubert," a gay voice
called.

In dire confusion Franz mumbled a perfunctory
"Guten Morgen, Gnädigste," and stepped back into

his room. Only later did he realize that this beautiful girl was the little Countess Karola herself.

Now Schubert's life, after the miserable months of illness and disappointment, took a happier turn. His health, in the pure country air, improved rapidly. He took long walks with the two young Countesses, and they treated him almost like a brother.

Karola, especially, was so kind that Franz soon lost his heart completely. In his saner moments he would realize how hopeless such a love must be, but after some especial favor which the fair young Countess tossed all unthinking in his way, Schubert would begin to think he might have some chance after all.

One evening while he was playing—lost in improvising magic harmonies from the deep emotion in his heart—he looked up to see Karola bending over the piano. Her dark eyes glowed with feeling.

"How beautiful!" she murmured. "That is the loveliest music I ever listened to. What is it called?"

Franz blushed in ecstatic confusion. "It has no name, Fräulein." His fingers went on weaving a soft pattern while he spoke. "It was only my heart," he added in a whisper, to himself, "speaking to you. . . ."

Karola smiled. "Then you must dedicate the piece to me," she said. "Why have you never inscribed any of your music in my name?"

Franz was still more confused. "Ah, don't you

know," he exclaimed fervently, "don't you know that everything I write is dedicated to you?"

The young Countess sighed. "You have a very deep-feeling nature, my friend," she said softly.

For a moment Schubert's heart beat madly, and his plain, round face shone with unhoped-for joy. He longed as never before in his life for words with which to express his emotions. But his elation did not last long.

"Herr Schubert is indeed an excellent *musician*," came a coldly ironical voice. Unnoticed by the young people, Count Esterházy had approached the piano and was standing just behind the luckless musician.

Suddenly, as Franz turned and saw the arrogant expression on the Count's face, his beautiful dream came tumbling down in shattered bits. He saw himself as he must appear to the Esterházys—a little, fat, snub-nosed, short-sighted, *paid* musician. How could he ever have presumed to think himself the equal of nobility?

He rose unsteadily to his feet. "If the *Herrschaften* will kindly excuse me," he said wearily, passing his hand over his forehead, "I—I have a headache, and I will beg permission to retire."

Franz went out into the garden and walked alone in the night. Darkness seemed to have intensified the scents of the flowers; the fragrance of lilacs, lilies, and mignonette was so compelling that it made him

think of the incense in the Church of St. Stephen.
He imagined to himself that he was in a cathedral—
the vast cathedral of nature, where stars take the place
of candles, and flowers of incense. In the stillness of
the night he could hear faint echoes of celestial music
sounding through the skies.

Suddenly he felt sorry for the people he had left
in the drawing-room. It was true that Count Esterházy and his family had everything in the way of
material luxury; yet it seemed to Schubert that in
spite of this they lived in poverty. For music, to
them, was only a pastime; they did not understand its
real meaning.

"Music," Franz thought to himself, "is truly the
wellspring of the spirit." Now he saw, as in a vision,
that those who live in communion with great harmonies are spiritually nourished, and that they who can
interpret this mighty language are lifted to the highest nobility of this earth.

Schubert went up to his room, lit a candle, and
began to write. Only a prayer—a prayer interpreted
through music—could express the exaltation in his
heart.
   "Ave Maria, ora pro nobis. . . ."

Dawn was just breaking when Franz finally un-
dressed and went to bed. As usual, he forgot to take
off his spectacles.

CHAPTER XVI

Moonshine House

WHEN Schubert returned to Vienna in
the fall of 1824, he was saddened to
find that three of his best friends had
moved away. Spaun was now in Linz
with his family; the talented young artist Kupelwieser
had gone to Rome; and Schober, dearest of them all,
had traveled north on a mysterious mission.

"You, dear Schober," Franz wrote to him, "I can
never forget, for no one else can ever be to me, alas,
what you once were." The separation was not for
long, however. Schober, it later came out, had decided to try his luck as an actor; but he had so little

255

success on the stage that after a few months he returned to Vienna.

Schubert's friends took the place of wife and
family, and he could not live without them.   From
Zelész he had written:

"If only we were together . . . but instead we
are all separated, each one in a different corner, and
in that lies my real unhappiness.   I want to cry out
with Goethe: 'Who will bring back one hour alone of
that most blessed time?'   That time when in our intimate circle each showed the other, with motherly
diffidence, the children of his Art, and waited, not
without apprehension, for the verdict that Love and
Truth would pronounce upon them; that time when
each inspired the other with a common striving towards the Ideal that animated all."

With Schober and Spaun gone, Franz turned now
for companionship to Moritz von Schwind—a seven-
teen-year-old artist who had recently joined the
"Schubertians".

Schwind was a gay, handsome, and precocious
boy, with intelligent eyes and an ardent, excitable nature.   He was a fair musician ("one must have at
least a mouthful of music every day," he said), but
had decided to make painting his career.   Eventually
Moritz von Schwind became one of Germany's best-
known artists; in a number of his pictures likenesses
of Schubert are to be found.

Moritz came to have a special place in Franz's heart. The two had a great deal in common; they both knew the meaning of artistic creation, and they could share impressions.

"In Schwind I find my fullest understanding," Schubert once said, and the young artist on his side remarked: "The more I become aware of what he [Schubert] is, the more I know what he suffers."

Schwind's family had lost most of their fortune, but they still owned an old rambling house next to the Karlskirche called the *Mondscheinhaus* (Moonshine House). In the garden at the back there was a small pavilion in which Moritz lived with his brothers, while his mother and sisters had their quarters in the larger house at the front.

The Schwinds were a very sociable family; their house was always filled with friends, and they had endless parties, dancing, and music. "No one who entered the house of that Schwind family," wrote one of their friends, "and took part in its revels could ever forget it, and everyone was compelled to admit that the like of it would never be seen again. . . ."

Franz found a welcome place in this group, and the "Schubertians" began to use the pavilion at the end of the garden as a meeting place. The atmosphere of "Moonshine House" appealed so much to

Schubert that on his return from Zelész he took rooms at a small inn next door to the Schwinds. From his window there he could look out over the garden, and the bells of the neighboring church made music for him night and day.

Moritz von Schwind was trying very hard at that time to establish himself as an artist. In his effort to make money for his family, he painted anything that would bring in a few gulden—Christmas cards, wedding-pictures, and even designs for tombstones. (In 1825 he did sixty of these last, Mayrhofer writing the epitaphs, which reflected the poet's gloomy temperament.)

One day Schubert came over to the pavilion of "Moonshine House" to take Moritz for a walk into the country. Schwind was working on a wedding-picture that had to be delivered that evening.

"I have nearly finished, Franz," he said. "Give me a few moments longer and I will be with you. Here—" he picked up a volume of Shakespeare that was lying on the table, "amuse yourself with this while you wait."

Schubert sat down quietly in a corner and began reading the book. Suddenly he started up with an exclamation.

"Here is something I have heard before," he said, trying to remember the circumstances. Then it all came back to him—that day in the country with Therese Grob, when they had listened to the meadow-larks, and she had recited Shakespeare's poem to him. He had never forgotten Therese—no other woman had ever meant so much to him.

"Hark! hark! the lark at heaven's gate sings," he read aloud; "and Phoebus 'gins arise. . . ."

Schubert began to hum a lilting melody. "Listen, Moritz, don't you hear?   It makes a song all by itself."   He fumbled in his pockets.   "Music-paper!   Why the devil do I never have music-paper when I need it?"

Schwind left his work with a laugh.   "You shall have music-paper as fast as I can draw the lines," he cried, seizing a ruler.

Now there was quiet in the little room of the "Moonshine" pavilion.   Each of the friends was en-grossed in creative work.   Schwind's was only a stupid wedding-picture, made to gratify the vanity of a wealthy burgher, and not an expression of a compelling inner urge.   But Franz Schubert's was a song for the ages.*

He had finished even before Moritz was through, and immediately had to sit down at the piano and play the new song.

* "Hark! Hark! the Lark" appealed so much to Liszt that he made a brilliant piano transcription of the song, which is a great favorite with concert players.

Allegretto

Hark! hark! the lark   at   heaven's gate sings, And

Phoe - bus   'gins   a - rise

Schwind was entranced. "This is one of the
finest things you have written, Franz." In later years
Schwind declared: "The lines that I drew for Schubert's 'Hark! Hark! the Lark' had more value than
any other drawing I ever did in my whole life."

"Have you something new for me to sing,
Franz?" asked Vogl one spring morning in 1825.

Schubert waved his hand towards a pile of
freshly written manuscript. "I have a new collection
—rather different from my other songs," he replied.
"You would never guess where I got the inspiration!"

Vogl looked through the music. "Scott's *Lady
of the Lake!*" He gave a low whistle of surprise.
"So you've taken to the English poets now. What's
this? 'Ave Maria' . . ."

Franz took the manuscript from Vogl and stared
at it for a moment without speaking. "Yes—it is
Ellen's song in that poem. The inspiration came to

me last summer in Zelész," he said.   "It was a melody
straight from heaven.   I hope," he added simply,
"that it will move others as it moved me."

Vogl was deeply impressed by the "Ave Maria",
and he was enthusiastic about the entire cycle from
The Lady of the Lake.

"You know," he exclaimed, "I think we should
go on another tour through Upper Austria this summer.   With these new songs of yours we could give
concerts as we go.   We could stop in Steyr and Linz,
and I have friends in Gmunden who have been beg-
ging me to bring you to visit them.   You would like
the Trawegers—they are cultivated, charming people,
and very musical as well."

Schubert and Vogl spent only two weeks in Steyr
this time.   As on their previous visit, they were
enthusiastically welcomed by Albert Stadler and his
family, Herr von Koller and the fair Pepi, and all
the other friends who had entertained them so gener-
ously before.   They would have remained longer if
they had not made plans to stop in Linz and Gmunden.

Franz had specially looked forward to seeing his
old comrade Spaun in Linz, but when he arrived, he
found to his dismay that his friend was not there.
Spaun had gone to Lemberg.   Schubert wrote to him
in great disappointment:

You can imagine how furious I am at having to write
a letter in Linz to you in Lemberg!!!   The devil take this

infamous Call of Duty that tears friends so cruelly apart when they have done no more than sip at the cup of friendship. Here I am sitting in Linz, sweating my heart out in this preposterous heat, a full folio of new songs with me—and you not there! Are you not ashamed of yourself? Linz without you is like a body without a soul, or a horseman without a head, or soup without salt. Were it not that Jägermeyr keeps such good beer, and that passable wine is to be found on the Schlossberg, I should really have to hang myself on the Promenade, with this superscription: "Died of grief for the fugitive soul of Linz!"

The Trawegers in Gmunden were even more congenial than Vogl had promised. Franz fell in love with the small son of the house, little Eduard, aged four. Children always adored Schubert—his own nature was so simple and childlike that he never failed to attract the younger members of the families that he visited.

The Trawegers' son was ill when the two musicians from Vienna arrived. The doctor had prescribed leeches, but the child screamed in rebellion whenever they approached him.

"Let me try," said Schubert in his gentle way. And to the surprise of the whole family, small Eduard grew suddenly quiet and docile.

Franz became the boy's greatest friend. In the morning, as soon as Eduard awoke, he would run in to Schubert's room in his nightshirt, and jump into bed with him. Vogl, next door, was not too pleased at the shrieks of laughter and uproarious play that roused everyone in the household.

When Schubert tired of playing he would take little Eduard on his knee. "Now you must learn to sing," he would say, solemn as a schoolmaster. Soon he had taught the boy several songs.

"Eduard, sing '*Guten Morgen*' and I will give you a shining penny."

"I squeaked as loudly as I could," young Traweger said, recounting the incident in later years.

There were many concerts during the visit in Gmunden. Vogl sang, and Schubert as usual accompanied him; the new song cycle was especially successful. To his parents, Franz wrote:

For six weeks I was in Gmunden, where the surrounding country, which is heavenly, touched me very deeply—as did also the inhabitants, particularly the good Trawegers— and did me a world of good. I was absolutely free at the Trawegers', just as if I were at home. . . . My new songs from Walter Scott's *Lady of the Lake* in particular had great success. There was a good deal of surprise too at my piety, which found expression in a hymn to the Blessed Virgin [*Ave Maria*], which seems to have moved all hearts and created quite a devotional effect. I fancy that this is because my religious feeling is never forced, and I never compose hymns or prayers of this sort unless I am involuntarily overcome by a sense of devotion, and then the feeling is, as a rule, genuine and heartfelt.

Schubert wrote long letters home about the beauties of the country he and Vogl visited on their trip through Upper Austria. He had always wanted to see Salzburg, the birthplace of Mozart, and now his long-dreamed-of wish came true.

The quaint city, surrounded by high, fantastic-looking mountains, made a vivid impression on Schubert. He wrote a detailed description of it to his brother Ferdinand:

It is almost impossible to give you any idea of the loveliness of the valley. You must imagine to yourself a garden, many miles in circumference, in which innumerable castles and estates peer out through or above the trees. Imagine a river, too, winding its serpentine course through meadows and fields like so many exquisitely colored carpets; excellent roads which twist ribbonlike about them; and finally vast avenues of gigantic trees: all this surrounded by an immense range of mountains, as though they were the guardians of this heavenly valley. Imagine all this and you will have a faint idea of its unspeakable beauty.

Schubert also told of visiting St. Peter's monastery, where Michael Haydn (Franz Josef's brother) had once lived.

Here, as you know [he continued], is M. Haydn's monument . . . I thought to myself: May your calm, clear spirit, good Haydn, rest upon me, and though I cannot ever be so quiet and so clear, yet certainly no one on earth reveres you more than I. (A slow tear fell from my eyes, and we went on farther.)

Good, honest Franz—so ready to recognize genius in others, and so reluctant to admit it in himself!

That same fall saw a joyous reunion of the
"Schubertians". For now Spaun returned to Vienna;
Kupelwieser came back from Rome, and Schober,
quite undisturbed by his failure to shine as an actor,
once more gladdened his friends with his gay personality. Then, to the surprise of everyone, Vogl married.

Vogl, who all his life had led a solitary, almost
ascetic existence, decided in his fifty-ninth year to
take a wife. She was much younger than he, in fact
she had been one of his pupils, and now sang in the
Vienna Opera. When Schubert's *Rosamunde* was
given a brief appearance in December of that year,
"Madame Vogl" was complimented on her singing
in the performance.

During the summers, when Schubert could get
into the country, his health always improved, but each
fall when he returned to Vienna he would again fall
ill. This time he was afflicted with a rash that made
all his hair fall out, and for a time he had to wear a
wig. Then once more he recovered, and his hair came
back in a mass of soft brown curls.

He decided now that it would be a good thing for him to secure a regular musical post. Salieri had recently died, and a musician named Eybler was appointed to fill his place as *Hof Kapellmeister*. Schubert applied for the post of assistant Kapellmeister. He sent the Emperor an elaborate petition in the style of the period:

Your Majesty!

Most gracious Emperor!

With the deepest submission the undersigned humbly begs Your Majesty graciously to bestow upon him the position of Vice-Kapellmeister to the Court, and supports his application with the following qualifications: [Here followed the list of qualifications.] . . .

Finally, he is at the present time without employment, and hopes in the security of a permanent position to be able to realize at last those high musical aspirations which he has ever kept before him.

Should Your Majesty be graciously pleased to grant this request, the undersigned would strive to the uttermost to give full satisfaction.

Your Majesty's most obedient humble servant,

FRANZ SCHUBERT

Vienna, 7th April, 1826

At the same time Schubert took a copy of one of his Masses to the new Kapellmeister Eybler.

"Eybler, when he heard my name," Schubert related, "said that he had not hitherto heard any of my compositions. I am not conceited, but I certainly

should have thought that by this time the Court Conductor of Vienna might have heard of me and my
work. When I came a few weeks later to inquire the
fate of my child, Eybler said that the Mass was good,
but not composed in the style which the Emperor
liked. I took my leave at once and thought to myself:
'So I am not fortunate enough to be able to compose
according to the style his Imperial Majesty ap-
proves!' "

Shortly after this, another position became avail-
able that was even more to Schubert's liking. The
Conductor of the Vienna Opera was transferred to
another city, and when Franz applied for the vacant
post his request was favorably considered. He was
told to compose a short dramatic work which he himself would direct as a test of his aptitude for the position.

The work was soon completed, and rehearsals
began. A Fräulein Schechner, one of the singers at
the Opera, was to take the soprano part. She was not
pleased with her role, and told Schubert he would
have to change some of the intervals.

"Very well, Fräulein," he said grudgingly, making the desired changes with evident ill-grace.

"And these notes in the Aria," the singer next
insisted, "they are much too high for anyone to
sing. . . ."

"*Wurz!*" ("rubbish") murmured Franz under his breath.

This time he refused to compromise. As the rehearsals progressed, the atmosphere grew tense. Schubert could not help seeing that the music was really beyond Fräulein Schechner's range, but now he had become stubborn, and refused to change a note.

"Let them find a singer that *can* sing it," he mumbled to himself.

At the final rehearsal three Kapellmeisters were present to judge the work and pass on Franz Schubert's ability as a possible conductor for the Vienna Opera.

The Overture went off in fine style. Franz conducted the orchestra and was quite pleased at the way his music sounded, while the visiting Kapellmeisters nodded their heads in approval. Everything progressed smoothly until the beginning of the soprano's Aria.

Fräulein Schechner made a great show of attempting the impossible. Finally she gave up and collapsed into a chair. The astounded orchestra gradually faded away into silence. . . .

Then everyone began to murmur with excitement. "Fräulein Schechner has ruined Schubert's music," his friends insisted. "Ridiculous!" exclaimed less partial listeners. "It is Herr Schubert who has tried to ruin the soprano's voice."

Several of the company went over and tried to make the young composer listen to reason. But Franz, usually so mild, was now roused to fury.

"No!" he exclaimed, closing the score with a bang. "I will change nothing!" And with this he stormed out of the theater—and away from all chances of Opera conductorship.

Schubert was very stubborn when it came to making changes in his music. He could not argue with his opponents, and so he would take refuge in silence, or an occasionally exploded "*Wurz!*"

Schindler, Beethoven's friend and biographer, said of Schubert: "One reason why Schubert's talent during his lifetime was mostly hidden under a bushel was a certain pig-headed obstinacy, an exaggerated sense of independence, which rendered him often deaf to the good and practical advice of well-intentioned friends."

When publishers asked him to send them music that would be easier to play, his reply was often to forward even more difficult compositions. And yet he seemed completely indifferent to praise. Schindler said that he never saw Schubert's expression change when anyone praised him.

Once, in a fashionable drawing-room, when the ladies had overwhelmed him with applause, he drew his friend Hüttenbrenner aside and whispered: "*Du!* I detest these women with their compliments. They understand nothing about music, and what they say to me they do not mean. Go, Anselm, and bring me, on the quiet, a little glass of wine."

When two professional orchestra players once approached Schubert in a tavern, and with all manner of flattery asked him to write some music for them, he replied curtly "No".

"But why not, Herr Schubert?" they insisted. "We are artists, you know, just as you are—"

Then Schubert exploded. "Artists! You call yourselves artists! Musical artisans! Nothing else. One bites into the mouthpiece of his wooden cudgel, and the other blows his cheeks out on a French horn. Do you call that *art?* A craft which brings in money, and there it ends. . . .

"Tootlers and fiddlers you are, all of you. *I* am an artist! *I*, I am Franz Schubert whom all the world knows and acclaims . . . and when the word 'artist' is mentioned it refers to me, not to you worms and insects. . . ."

It was very rarely, however, that Schubert lost his temper. That evening he had been drinking too much wine. The next morning he was completely penitent.

"I confess, I repent it. But I suppose I shall write the solos they asked me for, and then they will still kiss my hands for the gift. I know these people!"

Usually Schubert was the soul of modesty.   In his diary he wrote:

"With all my heart I hate that narrow-mindedness which makes so many wretched people believe that what they think and do is best, and that everything else is worthless.   One thing of beauty, it is true, should inspire a man throughout his life, yet the gleam of this single inspiration should illuminate everything else."

Music was the "single inspiration" of Franz Schubert's career, and it was destined to illuminate not only his own life, but millions of other existences.

CHAPTER XVII

"To Him Who Will Be Next"

"THE weather here is really terrible, and the Almighty seems to have forsaken us entirely," Schubert wrote from Vienna in the spring of 1826. "The sun refuses to shine. It is already May, and one cannot even sit in the garden. Fearful! Dreadful!! Appalling!!! For me the greatest cruelty one can imagine. . . . I am not working at all."

Sometimes Schubert wondered why he went on composing music. Certainly not for the money it brought him! The publishers were becoming more and more difficult to deal with. If he offered them a composition for one hundred florins (about $20) they were not content until they had beaten him down to a fraction of the amount. (For the last trio—one of his loveliest works, he was paid less than $5!) Schubert was too easy-going. He would accept anything if the bargainers held out long enough.

Yet he resented the advantage that was taken of him. "If only honest dealing were possible with these . . . publishers!" he wrote. "But the wise and beneficent regulations of our Government have taken good care that the artist shall remain the eternal slave of these miserable money-grabbers."

During Schubert's short lifetime (hardly thirteen years of actual work) he wrote close to two thousand compositions. His earnings for that entire period did not average over $240 a year. Living costs were of course much lower at that time, and this amount would have been sufficient to keep him from misery if he had not been so thoughtlessly generous as well as improvident. He was hardly ever free from debt, but as soon as he received a payment from his publishers he always settled first with his creditors. "He was absolutely honest, true, and upright," Hüttenbrenner said.

Schubert was never willing to write "pot-boilers". If the inspiration did not move him to compose, he simply waited until it came. For this reason very little of his music is of any but the highest quality.

Once when he was asked for an orchestral composition, which would have meant a well-paid commission, he replied:

"Since I possess nothing for full orchestra which I could send out with a quiet conscience into the world, and since there are so many selections from the great masters to choose from—for example Beethoven's Overtures, *Prometheus, Egmont, Coriolanus*, etc.,—I must heartily beg your forgiveness for not being able to help you in this matter, for it could only be prejudicial to me to appear with something mediocre."

"I think you should try other publishers," Schober insisted. Diabelli had just had the effrontery to offer less than fifteen florins (about $2.50) for a cycle of twelve songs (the "*Winterreise*"), and Schubert was beside himself.

"Certainly something must be done," he raged. "I work harder than ever and actually am earning less money than before." He had recently completed his string quartet called *Death and the Maiden*, the name being given because one of its themes is taken from Schubert's song of that title.

"There is Probst in Leipzig," suggested Schober. "It is a good, reputable firm. And Breitkopf and Härtel is another well-known house."

Schubert flung himself into a chair and took up his pen:

To the Publishers Breitkopf and Härtel in Leipzig.
Dear Sir:

In the hope that my name is not wholly unknown to you, I am venturing to ask whether you would be disposed to take over at a moderate price some of my compositions. . . .

He went on to enumerate the works he had on hand, and then drew out another sheet of paper.

To H. A. Probst in Leipzig.
Dear Sir:

In the hope that my name is not entirely unknown to you, I beg to put forward the proposal, which I trust may meet with your approval, . . .

When he had finished the two letters, Schubert sighed dismally. "Would you care to wager what their reply will be?"

Two weeks later Probst answered: "Though I thank you heartily for your confidence and assure you that I should be pleased to do my utmost to extend your reputation as an artist, I must confess that the somewhat unique expression of your genius and of your creations has interfered with their being generally understood and appreciated by our public. . . ."

Schubert had hoped to return to Gmunden that summer. The Trawegers had again invited him to visit them, and Franz anticipated a pleasant renewal of the previous year's agreeable association. But when the time came, he found he could not afford the journey.

"It is impossible for me to come to Gmunden or anywhere else, for I have absolutely no money, and everything else is going badly too," he wrote.

Schubert looked forward to his summer outings not only for the pleasure they brought him, but because his health was always improved in the country. He could no longer endure the hot weather in Vienna, and since he was unable to go to Upper Austria that year, he moved to the little village of Währing, just outside of Vienna. Here in ten days he wrote his last string quartet.

Schubert loved Nature with the instinctive devotion that a child feels for its mother, and from his long walks through forest and field he drew nourishment and inspiration for his music. The songs especially, with their fresh, romantic simplicity, bear the imprint of his communion with the world of Nature.

Early in the spring of 1827, it was rumored that Beethoven was seriously ill. One day there was a knock at Schubert's door, and when he opened it he found Schindler, the great composer's intimate friend.

Herr Schindler was plainly depressed. When

Franz inquired about Beethoven, he shook his head sadly.

"Every day he grows weaker, alas. Three times now the doctor has operated in an effort to relieve his dropsy, but it does no good. I fear he cannot last much longer."

Schubert was too moved to speak. He wondered what had brought Herr Schindler to his rooms.

"The master can no longer write music," his visitor went on, "but he seems to find great pleasure in looking through the works of others. He was recently sent a set of Handel's compositions * that gave him the greatest joy." Schindler fixed his sad eyes on Schubert. "He came across one of your songs the other day, and was greatly impressed. Do you know what he said?"

Franz waited eagerly to hear.

Schindler quoted: " 'Truly this Franz Schubert has the divine spark!' Those are the very words he used; and he asked me if I would bring him some more of your songs."

Schubert was deeply affected. He began hunting through his manuscripts, pulling out one song after another. "I wonder if he would like this?" and "here's one that might perhaps please him . . . or this . . . or this?"

---

* This volume of Handel's works is said to have been presented to Schubert after Beethoven's death.

When he had gathered a large portfolio of the songs, he handed them to Schindler.

"But you must take them yourself," the latter insisted. "Herr van Beethoven asked especially to see you."

Franz was quite overcome. All his life he had idolized the great master, never daring—in his humility—to hope that he would meet him personally. And now, in the last hours of Beethoven's life, he was to have this privilege. . . .

He went immediately with Schindler, and entered the sick-room on tiptoe—quite forgetting that the unfortunate Beethoven was completely deaf. Franz would never have recognized the gaunt, gray-haired man as the same powerfully built, shaggy-headed figure he had seen occasionally at the taverns.

Beethoven looked over Schubert's manuscripts with evident appreciation. "You will move the world with these songs," he said in a feeble voice. Then he added with a sad smile: "Perhaps more than my own music will . . . !"

Franz was sincerely shocked. Never for a moment had he imagined that his music could approach that of Beethoven—yet here was the great master himself making the comparison.

Beethoven died a short time later. They buried him in the cemetery of Währing, and Schubert was

chosen to be one of the torch-bearers at the funeral.
After the last rites were over, he returned to Vienna
and went with some friends to a tavern. They were
all very much subdued. When a bottle of wine was
opened, Franz proposed a melancholy toast:

"To him we have just buried!" he exclaimed.
Then added, raising his glass once more: "To him
who will be next!"

Schubert could not foresee that he was drinking
a toast to himself.

In Graz there lived a family by the name of
Pachler, whose greatest interest was in music. For
some years now Anselm Hüttenbrenner's headquar-
ters had been in Graz, and he had told the Pachlers a
great deal about Franz Schubert. In the summer of
1827, they invited the composer to spend several
weeks with them.

This was Franz's final journey away from
Vienna, and the last really happy period of his life.
Frau Pachler was an exceptionally good pianist; she
had been told by Beethoven that she played his compositions better than even the finest professionals.
The family felt honored to have Schubert with them,
and they did everything in their power to make his
visit pleasant.

They took him on excursions into the country—
long drives to the enchanting little castle of Haller
(in its courtyard there is now a tablet bearing the in-
scription: "In lasting remembrance of the Song
King"), and to Wildbach, the estate of Herr Pachler's aunt (where a portrait of Schubert was later put
up over the stable to commemorate his visit). There
were concerts and dances, amateur dramatics and
readings, merry companions and warm-hearted appreciation. Schubert wrote some of his finest dance
music during this visit.

At the suggestion of Anselm Hüttenbrenner he
had brought the score of *Alfonso and Estrella* to Graz.
The director of the opera was willing to produce it;
but when the orchestra started to decipher the score,
they insisted it was too difficult for them to play.

"Perhaps Herr Schubert would be willing to
simplify the music a little. . . . ?"

But Herr Schubert was not willing. He left the
manuscript with the Pachlers, and there it remained
for twenty-three years, until Schober, then living in
Weimar, unearthed the ill-fated opera and turned it
over to Franz Liszt.

Schubert was sorry to leave the agreeable life in
Graz. When he returned to Vienna he wrote to his
hostess:

I realize now that my life in Graz was far too pleasant,
and I am finding it very hard to settle down in Vienna again.

It is big enough, to be sure, but on the other hand it is devoid of open-heartedness and sincerity, of genuine ideas and sensible talk, and above all, of intellectual accomplishments. There is such a perpetual babel of small-talk here that it is difficult to know if one has a head on one's shoulders or not, and one rarely or never attains to any inward happiness. . . .

No sooner had Schubert established himself in Vienna again (this time with Schober at the "Blue Hedgehog") than he fell ill once more. He had a sudden, violent attack, with headaches and dizziness that made him almost blind. This eventually went away, but all his strength seemed gone and he was terribly depressed.

By nature Schubert was really a twofold being: while on the one side he was as gay and light-hearted as a child, on the other he could be as melancholy as his friend Mayrhofer. Perhaps the association with the poet brought out this side of his character, though more probably it was the result of his ill-health.

Now he was so despondent that he could no longer be persuaded to go to the tavern with his friends. He preferred staying at home and reading gloomy poetry. One day Spaun came in and found him with a collection of Wilhelm Müller's poems called *Winterreise*.

"Only listen to this, Josef," he said. "It is so sadly beautiful!" He read aloud:

"So now the last word's spoken,
    Myself soon out of sight,
    I leave this farewell token,
    Good-night, my dear, good-night."

"I have a strange feeling sometimes," Franz went on, "as if *my* 'farewell' were not far distant. It would be better so—otherwise what will become of me, the poor musician? When age comes on I may be compelled, like Goethe's harper, to 'steal to the doors and beg my bread'."

"What nonsense you are talking," Spaun exclaimed, with forced cheerfulness. "You are just at the beginning of life—thirty your last birthday. Come, come, don't dwell on such unhappy thoughts."

"I have been setting these poems to music," Franz went on, "and I'm anxious to know what you will think of them. They have affected me more deeply than any songs I ever composed."

Schubert played the *"Winterreise"* song cycle through for his friend; but Spaun thought the songs much too dismal.

"Ah, well," said Schubert, "they please me more than any I have written, and some day they will please you, too."

After the New Year Schubert was suddenly inspired to write another symphony. Six years had passed since the *Unfinished* was laid away and forgotten. This new symphony, Franz felt, would be his greatest work.

As if subconsciously he realized what a short time was left to him, he plunged into the work with a furious energy that drove him day and night. All of his powers seemed gathered together for a last, supreme effort, and this found expression in the great C-major Symphony—the crowning achievement of a richly creative life.

There are over two hundred pages in the manuscript of this work, and much of it was written with such compelling speed that the original score is almost illegible.

Spaun was concerned at the relentless way in which Schubert was driving himself. "You work too hard, Franz, and spend too many hours poring over your music-paper. You will exhaust yourself with such labor. . . ."

Schubert looked up at his friend with a gentle, singularly detached smile. "Oh, but no, my Josef. You do not understand. On the contrary, when I compose it is as if I received new strength—as if I were lifted up into a current of energy. Everything else is forgotten then; even I myself no longer exist." His eyes took on a faraway expression. "There is only music then—filling the air, pouring through my head and fingers . . . as if I were enveloped in a sea of sound."

As Franz tried to describe those radiant moments, his plain, round face grew strangely luminous. Then the light died away and he looked suddenly weary. "But afterwards," he continued in a dull voice, "I am very tired, and I remember that my body is ill and weary . . . that I have had nothing to eat for hours . . . that the room is damp and cold —in short, that I am thoroughly miserable."

The Vienna Musikverein planned to play the new Symphony at one of their spring concerts. But when it was put into rehearsal they decided that the work was too long, and too difficult for the players. So an earlier symphony—the other one in C major, written in 1818—was substituted.

The final C-major Symphony was played just once—a few weeks after Schubert's death—and then forgotten for eleven years, when Robert Schumann found the score and persuaded Mendelssohn to produce it in Leipzig. There it met with instant success.

Schubert knew that he had written a great work, and he was sadly disappointed at its apparent failure.

"So many of my works have never been performed, and there are dozens that I've never even heard!" he said, and added with unconscious pathos:

"The greatest joy for a composer is to hear his 'children' in actual sound. Ah, well—" he sighed and shrugged his shoulders as if dismissing an unworthy thought, "neither did the great Beethoven hear the vast creations of his later years. Who am I to complain? At least I have my hearing!"

CHAPTER XVIII

With Beethoven

THE spring and summer of 1828 came and went. Schubert made a few excursions into the country (a proposed trip to the Trawegers' again had to be given up because of "lack of funds"), wrote a few songs and began a new Mass. But he felt listless and lacking in ambition; he who had always loved life, laughter, and gay companions now felt curiously detached, as if he had done with trivial concerns.

When September came, Schubert decided to leave Schober and the "Blue Hedgehog", and go to his brother Ferdinand. The latter was now living in a suburb just outside of Vienna, and Franz hoped that the country air would improve his health and spirits.

Also he wanted to be with someone who was joined to him in blood relationship. Schubert had always felt nearer to Ferdinand than to any other living soul. "You are my closest friend, bound to me by every fiber of my being," he had once written to him.

Ferdinand was determined to restore his brother to health. "No more evenings at the tavern for you! —no more wine and heavy food," he insisted. "You must live a quiet life, with plenty of exercise. A few days of walking in the country would do you a world of good."

The two started off for a three-day walking tour. It was a tiring trip, and Schubert was quite worn out by the time they got back to Vienna. But he did feel a little better and worked again at his Mass.

On the last day of October, Franz with his brother and some other friends went to the *Rothenkreuz* (Red Cross) tavern for supper. Schubert ordered fish, but after he had taken a few mouthfuls he threw down his knife and fork.

"This fish is spoiled!" he cried, feeling suddenly ill; then he added in a panic: "I am poisoned. . . ."

Although there seemed to be no bad after-effects from this incident, from that moment Schubert ceased to have any appetite and ate practically nothing.

"It sometimes appears to me as if I belonged no more to this world," he told a friend.

And yet he did not suspect the real seriousness of his condition. He even decided he would take some lessons in fugue and counterpoint from a man named Sechtner who was reputed a great authority in the subject. Schubert went on foot all the way to Vienna to arrange for the lessons. It was a three-hour walk, and by the time he got back to Ferdinand's house he was completely exhausted and burning with fever.

Even then he would not stay in bed and insisted that it was only a passing indisposition; although he was taking no nourishment he could not understand why he was so weak. He had not seen Schober since moving to his brother's home. On October 12 he wrote to ask him for some books:

Dear Schober:

I am ill. I have had nothing to eat or drink for eleven days now, and can only wander feebly and uncertainly between armchair and bed. Rinna is treating me. If I take any food I cannot retain it at all.

So please be so good as to come to my aid in this desperate condition with something to read. I have read Cooper's *Last of the Mohicans, The Spy, The Pilot,* and *The Pioneers*. If by any chance you have anything else of his, I beg you to leave it for me at the coffee-house with Franz von Bogner. My brother, who is conscientiousness itself, will bring it over to me without fail. Or indeed anything else.

                    Your friend,
                                        Schubert

The days went by and Schubert grew steadily worse. At last he became so weak that he could no longer rise from his bed, and his little stepsister Josepha—a child of thirteen—devoted herself to his care. When Spaun came to visit him, Franz insisted fretfully: "There is nothing really the matter with me, but I am so weak that I feel I shall fall through the bed."

Schubert really had no fear of death. He had often in the past joked with Ferdinand, who always imagined he was going to die whenever he was ill.

As though dying were the worst evil we mortals had to face [he had written some years before in a letter to his parents]! If only he [Ferdinand] could see these marvelous mountains and lakes, whose aspect threatens to crush us or swallow us up, he would become less enamored of the tiny span of human life, and would be ready joyfully to give his body to the earth, to be quickened by its incomprehensible forces into new life.

Dr. Rinna did not seem especially alarmed at Schubert's condition, but, when a few days later Rinna himself fell ill, two other physicians were called in consultation, and they realized at once what a sick man their patient was. They diagnosed the case as a malignant form of typhus.

On November 14th a friend named Bauernfeld —one of the last of the "Schubertians"—called to see Franz.

When I visited Schubert for the last time [Bauernfeld wrote in his book *Alt Wien*], he was lying on his bed very ill. He complained of weakness and heat in the head, but he was still quite lucid and without any signs of delirium. Nevertheless the depressed spirits of my friend filled me with grave forebodings. His brother came with the doctors. By the time evening arrived the patient was wildly delirious. The most virulent form of typhus had manifested itself.

Schubert was out of his head most of the time during the following day.

"What are they doing with me?" he cried, struggling to get out of his bed.

Ferdinand tried to pacify him; but Franz continued to struggle. "Put me in my room," he begged. "Don't leave me in this corner under the earth. Don't I deserve a place above the ground?"

"You *are* in your own room," his brother reassured him in a soothing voice. "This is your own bed you are lying on. . . ."

"It is not true," the dying man gasped. "No— *Beethoven* is not here!"

Poor, unassuming Franz! During his lifetime he had never dared to think of Beethoven save on a pedestal far above his reach; but now, in death, he saw him as an equal.

Who shall say that he was not right? Franz Schubert's simple, heartfelt music has moved the hearts of many who yet could not understand the

mighty works of that other master.   And if it is
music's mission to bring comfort and joy, can anyone
doubt that Schubert may honorably stand beside the
greatest?

After Franz Schubert's death, the world began
to realize what a genius it had lost.   Everyone
mourned the tragedy that had cut off the young composer at so early an age; but there were those who—
considering the vast wealth of music which he left
behind him (few composers have exceeded this in
quantity, or quality!)—felt that he really compressed
a lifetime of achievement into the few years that were
allotted to him, and did indeed complete the work for
which he came into the world.

Living outwardly in misery and neglect, it was
Schubert's mission to create beauty from the inner
richness of his spirit.   He left a rare heritage for the
ages, inspiring the hearts of his fellowmen, and light-
ing their way to release from care and sorrow.

At Schubert's death his entire possessions were
valued at less than $15.   There were more than five
hundred manuscripts of unpublished music included,
the lot of them rated at a fraction over $2!   But in
1927 the score of one of his songs sold for $750—a
quarter the amount of his total life earnings.

Ferdinand insisted, because of his brother's dying words, that Franz must be buried beside Beethoven in the Währing cemetery. Schober designed the headstone of his grave, and Grillparzer wrote the epitaph:

Music has here buried a rich treasure,
But much fairer hopes.

Franz Schubert lies here.
Born January 31, 1797.
Died November 19, 1828.
31 years old.

SCHUBERT	BEETHOVEN (b. 1770)
	1792 — Goes to Vienna to live.
1797 — Birth at Lichtenthal, Austria.	1800 — First Symphony performed.
1803 — At six, begins piano study.	1801 — Deafness increasing. 1803 — *Kreutzer* Sonata performed. 1804 — Third (*Eroica*) Symphony performed.
1805 — Begins violin lessons.	1805 — First performance of *Fidelio*.
1808 — Admitted to the Konvikt. 1809 — Becomes first violinist of the Konvikt orchestra.	1807 — Fourth Symphony and *Coriolanus* Overture performed. 1808 — Fifth and Sixth Symphonies finished. 1810 — First performance of the *Egmont* Overture.
1811 — Composes *Hagar's Lament*. 1813 — Leaves the Konvikt. Composes his First Symphony in D. 1814 — Starts teaching at his father's school. Composes *Gretchen am Spinnrade* and many other works. 1815 — Many compositions, including *Der Erlkönig* and *Heidenröslein*.	1812 — Seventh and Eighth Symphonies finished. 1814 — First performance of the Eighth Symphony. 1815 — Is given the freedom of the city of Vienna.
1816 — Goes to live with Schober. Songs include *Der Wanderer*. 1818 — With the Esterházys at Zelecz. 1819 — The *Trout* Quintet composed. 1820 — Production of *Die Zwillingsbrüder* and *Die Zauberharfe*.	1817 — Ninth (*Choral*) Symphony begun. 1818 — *Missa Solemnis* begun.
1821 — *Der Erlkönig* first sung in public. 1822 — Finishes *Alfonso and Estrella*. Calls at Beethoven's house. 1823 — *Rosamunde* music performed. Composes the *Schöne Müllerin* cycle and other songs.	1823 — Ninth Symphony finished. 1824 — Ninth Symphony and *Missa Solemnis* performed.
1826 — Composes the B-flat Trio and many songs including "Who is Sylvia?" and "Hark! Hark! the Lark." 1827 — Completes the *Winterreise* cycle and writes the E-flat Trio. 1828 — Completes the great C-major Symphony and the *Schwanengesang* cycle. Dies on November 19.	1826 — The "Last Quartets" finished. 1827 — Death, March 26.

OTHER MUSICAL EVENTS	NON-MUSICAL EVENTS
1791 — Mozart d. Paradies d. Meyerbeer b. Czerny b.	1790 — Benjamin Franklin d.
1792 — Rossini b. Lowell Mason b.	1792 — Eli Whitney invents the cotton gin. John Paul Jones d. Sir Joshua Reynolds d.
1797 — Donizetti b. Haydn composes *The Creation* and the *Emperor* Quartet.	1797 — Heine b.
1800 — Haydn composes *The Seasons.*	1799 — George Washington d. Balzac b.
	1800 — Macaulay b. Cowper d.
1801 — Cimarosa d. Bellini b.	1801 — Farragut b. Seward b.
	1802 — Hugo b. Dumas (*père*) b.
1803 — Berlioz b.	1803 — Louisiana Purchase. Emerson b.
1804 — At 72, Haydn is made an honorary citizen of Vienna. Johann Strauss the Elder b. Glinka b.	1804 — Hawthorne b. Disraeli b. Hamilton killed by Aaron Burr in a duel.
1805 — Boccherini d.	1805 — Battle of Trafalgar. Lord Nelson d. Hans Christian Andersen b.
	1807 — Garibaldi b. Robert E. Lee b. Longfellow b.
	1808 — Jefferson Davis b.
1809 — Haydn d. Mendelssohn b.	1809 — Trial of Aaron Burr for treason. The French occupy Vienna. Births of Lincoln, Gladstone, Poe, Darwin, Holmes, and Tennyson.
1810 — Chopin b. Schumann b. Ole Bull b.	1810 — P. T. Barnum b.
1811 — Liszt b.	1811 — Thackeray b. Horace Greeley b.
1812 — Flotow b.	1812 — Dickens b. Browning b. Edward Lear b. H. B. Stowe b. Retreat of Napoleon's army from Moscow. War begins between England and the United States.
1813 — Grétry d. Wagner b. Verdi b. The Royal Philharmonic Society is founded in London.	1813 — David Livingstone b.
1814 — The first singing of *The Star-Spangled Banner* (Baltimore).	1814 — Stephenson invents the locomotive.
	1815 — Robert Fulton d. Bismarck b. Battle of Waterloo. Bonaparte is exiled to St. Helena.
1816 — Rossini's *The Barber of Seville* has its first performance.	1816 — Charlotte Brontë b.
	1817 — Jane Austen d. Thoreau b. Whittier b.
1818 — Gounod b.	1818 — Karl Marx b. George Rogers Clark d.
1819 — Offenbach b. Clara Schumann b.	1819 — Walt Whitman b. Lowell b. Ruskin b. George Eliot b. Queen Victoria b.
1820 — Jenny Lind b. Vieuxtemps b.	1820 — Florence Nightingale b. George III d.
1821 — First performance of Weber's *Der Freischütz.*	1821 — Napoleon Bonaparte d. Keats d. Clara Barton b. Flaubert b.
1822 — Franck b.	1822 — Shelley d. Pasteur b. Grant b.
1823 — Rossini's *Semiramide* performed. *Home, Sweet Home* first sung at a performance of the opera *Clari* in London. Lalo b.	1823 — Monroe Doctrine announced.
1824 — Bruckner b. Smetana b.	1824 — Byron d. Stonewall Jackson b. Dumas (*fils*) b.
1825 — Johann Strauss the Younger b.	1825 — Erie Canal finished. T. H. Huxley b.
1826 — Weber d. Mendelssohn composes his *Midsummer Night's Dream* Overture. Stephen Collins Foster b.	1826 — Thomas Jefferson d. John Adams d. Empress Eugénie b.
	1827 — Lister b.
	1828 — Tolstoi b. D. G. Rossetti b.

FRANZ SCHUBERT'S COMPOSITIONS

NOTE—*The complete list of Schubert's works is too long to print here, and only the most important are therefore given. Of these, nearly all have been recorded, in whole or in part. For exact information about recordings, consult a music dealer.*

OPERAS, OPERETTAS, AND INCIDENTAL MUSIC

> *Des Teufels Lustschloss,* 1813-14
> *Die Zwillingsbrüder,* 1819
> *Die Zauberharfe,* 1820
> *Alfonso and Estrella,* 1821-22
> *Rosamunde von Cypern,* 1823

SYMPHONIES

No. 1, D major, 1813
No. 2, B flat major, 1815
No. 3, D major, 1815
No. 4, C minor (*Tragic*), 1816
No. 5, B flat major, 1816
No. 6, C major, 1818
No. 7, C major, 1828 (the great C-major symphony, sometimes called No. 9)
No. 8, B minor (*Unfinished*), 1822

OTHER ORCHESTRAL WORKS

> Eight Overtures
> *Concertstück* for violin and orchestra, 1816
> Five German Dances, 1813
> Five Minuets (*Deutsche*), 1813

CHAMBER MUSIC

Sonata in A for piano and violin, Opus 162, 1817
Sonatina in D for piano and violin, Opus 137, No. 1, 1816

Sonatina in A minor for piano and violin, Opus 137, No. 2, 1816
Sonatina in G minor for piano and violin, Opus 137, No. 3, 1816

String Trio in B flat (violin, viola, 'cello), 1817
Piano Trio in B flat, Opus 99, 1826
Piano Trio in E flat, Opus 100, 1827

String Quartet No. 1 in B flat, 1812
String Quartet No. 2 in C, 1812
String Quartet No. 3 in B flat, 1812
String Quartet No. 4 in C, 1813
String Quartet No. 5 in B flat, 1813
String Quartet No. 6 in D, 1813
String Quartet No. 7 in D, 1814
String Quartet No. 8 in B flat, Opus 168, 1814
String Quartet No. 9 in G minor, 1815
String Quartet No. 10 in E flat, Opus 125, No. 1, 1817
String Quartet No. 11 in E, Opus 125, No. 2, 1817
String Quartet No. 12 in C minor (the *Quartettsatz*), 1820
String Quartet No. 13 in A minor, Opus 29, 1824
String Quartet No. 14 in D minor (*Death and the Maiden*), 1826
String Quartet No. 15 in G, Opus 161, 1826

Quintet in A for piano, violin, viola, 'cello, and double bass (*Trout*),
    Opus 114, 1819
Quintet in C for 2 violins, viola, and 2 'cellos, Opus 163, 1828
Octet in F for 2 violins, viola, 'cello, double bass, clarinet, bassoon,
    and horn, Opus 166, 1824

PIANO WORKS

Sonata in A, Opus 120, 1825
Sonata in A, 1828
Sonata in A minor, Opus 42, 1825
Sonata in A minor, Opus 143, 1823
Sonata in A minor, Opus 164, 1817
Sonata in A flat, 1817
Sonata in B, Opus 147, 1817
Sonata in B flat, 1828
Sonata in C (unfinished) 1825

Sonata in C minor, 1828
Sonata in D, Opus 53, 1825
Sonata in E (unfinished), 1815
Sonata in E flat, Opus 122, 1817
Sonata in E minor (one movement), 1817
Sonata in G major, Opus 78, 1826
Seven other sonatas
Valses nobles, Opus 77
Valses sentimentales, Opus 50
Walzer, Ländler, und Ecossaisen, Opus 18, 1821
Deutsche und Ecossaisen, Opus 33, 1824
Wanderer Fantasy, Opus 15, 1822
Damenländler und Ecossaisen, Opus 67
Grätzer Walzer, Opus 91, 1827
Four Impromptus, Opus, 142, 1827
Four Impromptus, Opus 90, 1828
Klavierstücke, 1828
Moments musicaux, Opus 94, 1828 (?)
Twelve *Ländler,* Opus 171
Adagio and Rondo in E, Opus 145, 1817
Allegretto in C minor, 1828
Andante in C, 1812

PIANO, FOUR HANDS

Three *Marches militaires,* Opus 51
Three *Marches héroïques,* Opus 27
Divertissement à la hongroise, Opus 54
Divertissement on French themes, Opus 63
Children's March in G, 1827
Four Fantasies
Four *Ländler,* 1824
Marche héroïque for Nicholas I, Opus 66, 1826
Six Marches, Opus 40
Marches caractéristiques, Opus 121
Six Overtures
Ten Polonaises
Three Rondos

Sonata in B flat, Opus 30, 1824
Sonata in C (*Grand Duo*), Opus 140, 1824
Trauermarsch for Alexander I, Opus 55, 1825
Variations—Opus 10, 1818; Opus 35, 1824; Opus 82, No. 1, 1827

CHORAL WORKS

Cantatas for mixed voices, unaccompanied or with piano or orchestra
Songs for male voices, unaccompanied or with piano or orchestra
Songs for female voices

SONG CYCLES

Die Schöne Müllerin, 1823. Twenty songs including *Das Wandern*
(Wandering), *Wohin?* (Whither?), *Am Feierabend* (Holiday
Eve), *Ungeduld* (Impatience), and *Morgengrüss* (Morning
Greeting)

Winterreise, 1827. Twenty-four songs including *Gute Nacht*
(Good Night), *Der Lindenbaum* (The Linden Tree), *Auf
dem Flusse* (On the River), *Rückblick* (Retrospect), *Früh-
lingstraum* (Spring Dream), *Einsamkeit* (Loneliness), *Die Post*
(The Post), *Die Krähe* (The Crow), *Der Leiermann* (The
Organ Grinder), and *Das Wirtshaus* (The Inn)

Schwanengesang, 1828. Fourteen songs including *Liebesbotschaft*
(Love's Message), *Aufenthalt* (Delay), *Der Doppelgänger*
(The Double), *Die Taubenpost* (The Carrier Pigeon), *Am
Meer* (By the Sea), and *Das Fischermädchen* (The Fisher-
maiden)

SONGS NOT IN CYCLES

Of separate songs composed by Schubert there are several hun-
dred—too many to name here. For a complete list see the article
"Schubert" in Grove's *Dictionary of Music and Musicians* or *The
International Cyclopedia of Music and Musicians.*

Following are some of the most famous of these songs:

Die Allmacht (The Omnipotent)
Am See (By the Sea)
An die Laute (To the Lute)

An die Leier (To the Lyre)
An die Musik (To Music)
Auf dem Wasser zu singen (Singing on the Water)
Ave Maria—Ellen's song from *The Lady of the Lake*
Du bist die Ruh' (Thou art repose)
Der Erlkönig (The Erl-King)
Der Fischer (The Fisherman)
Die Forelle (The Trout)
Frühlingsglaube (Faith in Spring)
Geheimnis (Secrecy)
Gretchen am Spinnrade (Gretchen at the Spinning-Wheel)
Hark! Hark! the Lark
Heidenröslein (Hedge Rose)
Der Hirt auf dem Felsen (The Herdsman on the Cliff)
Im Abendroth (At Dusk)
Litanei (Litany for All Souls' Day)
Lob der Thränen (Praise of Tears)
Die Mainacht (May Night)
Mignon's Song [three by this title]
Nacht und Träume (Holy Night)
Rastlose Liebe (Restless Love)
Sei mir gegrüsst (Greeting)
Ständchen (Serenade)
Der Tod und das Mädchen (Death and the Maiden)
Der Wanderer (The Wanderer)
Who Is Sylvia?
Wiegenlied (Cradle Song: *"Schlafe, schlafe"*)

READING LIST

(A selected list of books dealing with Schubert and his works)

BATES, RALPH. Franz Schubert. Appleton, N. Y. 1935.

BIE, OSCAR. Schubert the Man. Dodd, Mead, N. Y. 1928.

BROWER, HARRIETTE M. Story Lives of Master Musicians. Stokes, N. Y. 1922.

CAPELL, RICHARD. Schubert's Songs. Benn, London. 1928.

CHAPIN, ANNA ALICE. Masters of Music, Their Lives and Works. Dodd, Mead, N. Y. 1923.

DEUTSCH, OTTO ERICH, ed. (transl. by V. SAVILE). Franz Schubert's Letters and Other Writings. Knopf, N. Y. 1928.

DUNCAN, EDMONDSTOUNE. Schubert. Longmans, London. 1869.

FLOWER, WALTER NEWMAN. Franz Schubert, the Man and His Circle. Stokes, N. Y. 1928.

FROST, H. F. Franz Schubert (in The Great Musicians series). Scribner's, London. 1881.

GILBERT, ARIADNE. Over Famous Thresholds. Century, N. Y. 1931.

GROVE, SIR GEORGE. Article "Schubert" in *Grove's Dictionary of Music and Musicians*. Macmillan, N. Y. 1935.

HADOW, W. H., ed. Oxford History of Music—vol. V, Viennese Period. Oxford, N. Y. 1931.

KOBALD, KARL. Franz Schubert and His Times. Knopf, N. Y. 1928.

KREISSLE VON HELLBORN. The Life of Franz Schubert. Longmans, London. 1869.

LE MASSENA, CLARENCE. The Songs of Schubert. Schirmer, N. Y. 1928.

MASON, DANIEL GREGORY. The Romantic Composers. Macmillan, N. Y. 1924.

PEYSER, HERBERT F. Article "Schubert" in *The International Cyclopedia of Music and Musicians*. Dodd, Mead, N. Y. 1938.

SCHWIMMER, FRANCISKA. Great Musicians as Children. Doubleday, N. Y. 1929.

SMITH, HANNAH. Founders of Music. Schirmer, N. Y. 1903.

TAPPER, THOMAS. First Studies in Music Biography. Presser, Phila. 1900.

WHEELER (OPAL) and DEUCHER (SYBIL). Franz Schubert and His Merry Friends. Dutton, N. Y. 1939.

INDEX

army, Austrian, 103
Austria-Hungary, 167

Bauernfeld, 291-92
Beethoven, 20, 21, 47-48, 57-58, 119, 142, 162, 221, 226, 237-39, 248, 274, 276-81, 292, 294; *Eroica* Symphony, 75
Brahms, 226
Breitkopf and Härtel, 157-58, 274, 275

Cooper's novels, 290
Czerny, Carl, 75

Diabelli, 223, 226, 246, 274
Dräxler, *Prometheus*, 151

Eckel, Franz, 51, 60-61, 62
Emperor, Austrian, 266-67
Empire, the, 167
Esterházy, Count, and his family, 166-81, 182-85, 249-54
Esterházy, Karola, 169, 170, 176, 179-80, 182, 251-53
Esterházy, Maria, 169, 170
Esterházy, Count Stefan, 183-85
Esterházy, Prince, 21, 166
Eybler, Kapellmeister, 266-67

Fröhlich sisters, 217-20, 227-36

Gluck, *Iphigenia in Tauris*, 136-37
Goethe, 191-94, 256; poems, 124-25, 143-45, 190
Gosmar, Luise, 228, 230, 234, 235, 236
Grillparzer, 218, 220, 221, 223, 228, 233, 234, 294

Grob, Therese, 119-22, 124, 125-31, 132-33, 142, 259
Grobs, the, 116-22, 123, 125-26, 132
Grove, George, 246-47
gypsy music, 25-26, 172, 179

Haller castle, 282
Handel, 277
Haydn, Franz Josef, 20, 21, 142, 166, 221, 264
Haydn, Michael, 264
Herbeck, 246
Hofmann, *Die Zwillingsbrüder*, 195
Holzapfel, Anton, 5, 11, 12-15, 51, 59-60, 62, 72, 74-78, 93, 105, 112, 113, 190
Holzer, Michael, 7, 9, 10, 21, 22, 28-33, 36, 38, 41-43, 46, 47, 115-17, 118, 119, 122
house signs, 35, 45
Hungarian music, 172
Hüttenbrenner, Anselm, 138-39, 141-42, 163, 164, 170, 188, 208, 209, 212, 225, 228, 237, 244-46, 269-70, 281
Hüttenbrenner, Josef, 138-39, 141-42, 163-64, 187, 188, 215-16, 247-48

Imperial Chapel Choir, 1, 3, 4, 6-7, 33, 49-50, 98-100

Kleyenbock, Anna, *see* Schubert, Anna
Koller family, 202, 203, 205, 261
Konvikt school, 1-16, 33, 37, 38, 49-102, 146; orchestra, 12, 50-55, 70

Kupelwieser, Leopold, 228, 232, 249, 255, 265

Laibach, School of music at, 131-32
Lang, Director, 1-2, 4, 7, 8, 10, 57, 59, 67, 68, 69, 71, 72, 88, 89, 99-100, 104, 105
Lichnowsky, Prince, 166
Lichtenthal school, 4, 17, 19, 26-27, 34-35, 37-38, 42-43, 108-12, 141, 240
Liszt, 259, 282

Mayrhofr, Johann, 113, 119, 121-22, 134-40, 141-42, 162, 171, 173, 186-87, 188, 189, 258
Mendelssohn, 286
Milder, Anna, 136-37, 139
Mozart, 20, 21, 52, 56, 70, 137, 221, 264
Müller's *Winterreise*, 283-84
music-paper, 46, 58-59, 61, 95, 259
music publishers, 157-58, 226-27, 248, 273-75

Napoleon, 41, 65-78, 167
Nepomuk, Bishop, 212, 213

Pachler family, 281-82
Paumgartner, 201, 203, 204
Peters, music publisher, 248
Probst, music publisher, 274, 275
Pyrker, Ladislaus, 225

Rinna, Dr., 291
Rossini, *The Barber of Seville*, 161
Rudolph, Archduke, 68-69
Ruziczka, Wendel, 8, 50-55, 79-87, 99, 146-48

Salieri, Antonio, 8-9, 12, 80-87, 89, 90, 102, 106, 108, 119,

121, 122, 124-25, 131, 167, 190, 194, 221, 266
Salzburg, 264
Schechner, Fräulein, 267-68
Schellman, Albert, 201, 203
Schindler, Anton, 238, 269
Schober, Franz von, 138-39, 146, 149, 153-56, 159, 165, 172, 173, 188, 198, 212, 213, 214, 219, 225, 228, 229, 237, 255, 265, 282, 283, 288, 290, 294
Schönstein, Baron, 169, 171-72, 222, 223
Schröder-Devrient, 193
Schubert, Anna, 101-102, 109, 137, 155
Schubert, Elisabet, 17-22, 25, 26, 34-43, 95-96, 101, 104
Schubert, Ferdinand, 19, 27, 36, 37, 44, 47, 92, 102, 103, 174, 180, 215, 240, 288-91, 294
Schubert, Franz, of Dresden, 157-58
Schubert, Franz Peter
  birth, 2, 20; home and childhood, 17-23, 25-33, 34-48; home music, 21, 47-48, 96-97; early love of music, 22, 25-26, 27-28; music lessons, 28-32; early composing, 15, 36, 45-46, 48, 58, 61-63, 80, 89, 91, 94, 112
  at the Konvikt, 1-16; his uniform, 12, 83; in the Music Room, 15-16, 48, 49-64, 79-105; in the orchestra, 50-55; made concertmaster, 80; becomes Salieri's pupil, 80-87; forbidden his home, 91-93; leaves the Konvikt, 102; at St. Anna's, 104-108; teaches school, 108 ff., 141, 153-54
  first love affair, 128-31, 132-33; applies for Laibach post, 131-32; further compositions, 142-

48; works at Schober's, 149; gives up teaching and goes to Schober's to live, 154-55; has a work performed publicly, 162; first publication, 162 with the Esterházys at Zelész, 166-81; back in Vienna, 182; moves to Mayrhofr's, 186; sends songs to Goethe, 191-93; visit to Steyr, 197-206; to Linz, 206; at production of *The Twins*, 207-10; commissioned to write *Zauberharfe*, 211; to St. Pölten, 212-13; moves to Schober's, 214 visits the Fröhlichs, 217-20, 227-35; and the Sonnleithners, 221-24; his songs printed, 223-24; dedications, 225; calls on Beethoven, 237-39; writes the *Unfinished*, 243-46; illness, 247-49; at Zelész again, 249-54; in Vienna, visits the Schwinds, 256-60; trip to Steyr, Linz, Gmunden, and Salzburg, 261-64

applies for post of asst. Kapellmeister, 266-67; for post at Vienna Opera, 267; tested as conductor, 267-69; moves to Währing, 276; visits the dying Beethoven, 278; at Beethoven's funeral, 281; visit to Graz, 281; last illness, 289-93; burial, 294

speed as composer, 124-25, 131, 215; prolific, 161, 225; dating his scores, 124; careless with his mss., 163; "buried" scores discovered, 246-47

poverty, 153, 165-66, 211, 226, 272-74, 288, 293; health, 214, 247-49, 265, 283, 289; eyesight and spectacles, 22, 103, 140, 254; dissipations, 156, 189, 214, 289

temperament, 269-70; stubbornness, 268-70; opinion of "artists," 270; nicknames, 190; dreams, 240-42; "My Dream," 241-42

compositions:
Alfonso and Estrella, 212, 213-14, 282
Am See, 113; first sung, 119
Ave Maria, 260-61
Death and the Maiden, 274
Ecossaises, 150
Einsamkeit, 171, 173
Ellen's songs from *The Lady of the Lake*, 260-63
Erlkönig, 144-48, 157-58, 159, 203, 222-25
Fantasia, 238
German Dances, 150
Gretchen at the Spinning-Wheel, 124, 224, 233
Hagars Klage, 80, 87, 88, 89
Hark! Hark! The Lark, 129, 259-60
Heidenröslein, 143, 233
Italian Overture, 162
Mass in F, 120-21, 122
Prometheus, 151-52, 222
Rastlose Liebe, 143
Requiem Mass, 174, 180
Rosamunde, 211, 247, 265
Sakuntala, 212
Ständchen, 233-36
Symphonies: #4, 161; #5, 161; #6, 161, 286; #7, 284-86; #8 (*Unfinished*), 243-46
Teufels Lustschloss, 106-107, 108, 120
Trauerwalz, 162-63, 227
Trout, song, 164; quintet, 204-205
Twins, 195-96, 207-10

Schubert, Franz Peter, compositions
(Cont.)
   Vatermörder, 94
   Wanderer, 226, 233
   Winterreise, 274, 283-84
   Zauberharfe, 211
Schubert, Franz Theodor, 2, 3, 4,
   17-20, 27, 28, 29, 31, 36, 38,
   42-48, 90-93, 96-97, 100-104,
   108, 109, 112, 115, 122-23,
   154, 240, 245
Schubert, Ignatz, 18-19, 27, 28,
   32, 37, 44, 47, 102, 103, 173,
   240
Schubert, Josepha, 291
Schubert, Karl, 19, 36, 37, 44-45,
   47, 95, 102, 103, 108, 109,
   154-55, 240
Schubert, Theresa, 27, 37, 44, 48,
   101, 102
"Schubertiades," 227-28
"Schubertians," 142, 144, 151,
   152, 188, 189, 208, 209-10,
   227, 228, 257, 265
Schumann, 286
Schwind family, 257
Schwind, Moritz von, 256-60
Scott's *Lady of the Lake*, 260-61,
   263
Sechtner, 290
Senn, Michael, 59-60, 67, 93, 173,
   188, 228
Shakespeare, *Hark! hark! the lark*,
   129, 259-60
Sonnleithner, Ignatz, 221-24
Sonnleithner, Leopold, 152, 217-
   19, 221-22, 228, 234

Spaun, Josef, 5-6, 52-53, 56-59,
   60, 61, 62, 80, 94-95, 106-107,
   134-41, 142, 144, 146, 147,
   149-51, 156-57, 173, 188, 191-
   93, 206, 225, 255, 261, 265,
   283-84, 285
Spina, music publisher, 246-47
Stadler, Albert, 93, 94, 112, 113,
   188, 198, 201, 205, 261
Stadler, Kathi, 202, 206
St. Anna's college, 104-108
St. Stephen, Cathedral of, 23, 73,
   254
Styrian Music Society, 245
Sullivan, Arthur, 246-47
Swiss Family, The, 106

Traweger family, 261-63, 275,
   288

Vienna, 21, 23-25, 41-42, 65-78
Vienna Musikverein, 286
Vienna Opera, 267-69
Vietz, Elisabeth, *see* Schubert,
   Elisabeth
Vogl, Johann Michael, 136-37,
   139, 158-61, 171, 191, 194-
   96, 197-206, 207, 208, 225,
   228, 229, 233, 260-63, 265

Walch, Prefect, 11, 59, 68, 71,
   72, 88
Watteroth, Prof., 149, 151-52,
   166, 222
Wienerwald, 25, 126

Zelész, 166-81, 250-54